Vocational Business

+
Market Research

Roger Lewis & Roger Trevitt

Published in 2003 by:
Nelson Thornes Ltd
Delta Place
27 Bath Road
CHELTENHAM
GL53 7TH
United Kingdom

03 04 05 06 07 / 10 9 8 7 6 5 4 3 2 1

A catalogue record for this book is available from the British Library

ISBN 0 7487 7108 5

Illustrations by Oxford Illustrators

Page make-up by GreenGate Publishing Services

Printed and bound in Croatia by Zrinski

Contents

Introduction to Vocational Business series

This textbook is one of a series covering the core areas of business studies. The first six books in the series cover the core units of the Business AVCE. A further five books look at the most popular optional units. Each book focuses on vocational aspects of business, rather than theoretical models, allowing the reader to understand how businesses operate. To complement this vocational focus, each book contains a range of case studies illustrating how businesses respond to internal and external changes.

The textbooks are designed to support students taking a range of business courses. While each is free standing, containing the essential knowledge required by the various syllabuses and course requirements, together they provide a comprehensive coverage of the issues facing both large and small businesses in today's competitive environment.

Titles in the series

Book 1   Business at Work
Book 2   The Competitive Business Environment
Book 3   Marketing
Book 4   Human Resources
Book 5   Finance
Book 6   Business Planning

Optional Units: Financial Accounting
                        Market Research
                        Marketing and Promotional Strategy
                        Training and Development
                        Business and the European Union

Acknowledgements

The authors and publishers would like to thank the following organisations for permission to reproduce material in this book: Advertising Standards Association (pages 10–11); CACI Market Analysis Ltd (pages 9 and 23); Coca-Cola (page 10); Colonise (page 25); Corel 62 (NT) (page 15); Croydon Market Research Centre (pages 27–28); Paul Jardine (page 46); The Office for National Statistics (pages 46 and 56); The Market Research Society (pages 22, 82 and 85); PACHA, London (page 7); Proctor and Gamble (page 38); Sainsburys (page 13); Target Group Index: BRMB International (pages 58–59); and UK 2000 Time Use Survey/HHSA Estimates (pages 55–56).

The authors would also like to thank the following people for their support and encouragement with this text: the team at Nelson Thornes, in particular Jane Cotter and Fiona Elliott; Liz Brereton at GreenGate; our colleagues and students; and finally, our families, once again.

Every effort has been made to contact copyright holders, and we apologise if any have been overlooked.

Market research

Introduction

Welcome to *Market Research*, which has been written specially to cover the syllabuses for the following examination boards (see Table 1):

Table 1 *Examination board syllabuses*

Examination Board	Unit	How assessed
Edexcel	Unit 8 Marketing Research	Mini case study given on the day. External examination 2 hours
OCR	Unit 7 Market Research	Prereleased case study material. External examination 1 hour 30 minutes
AQA	Unit 17 Market Research	Through a portfolio based on a market research survey

It also covers other syllabuses, e.g. OCR Cambridge Business Skills.

What would you like to know about yourself? Give us your postcode and we will tell you! Or look at page 8 and try the exercise for yourself. Market research is all around you, on Internet sites with pop-up questionnaires, your e-mail and fax machine, in the street and on the plane when you return from your package holiday (see Figure 1):

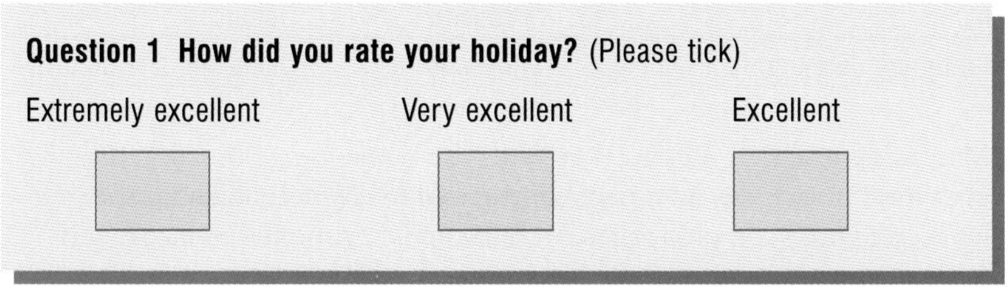

Question 1 How did you rate your holiday? (Please tick)

Extremely excellent   Very excellent   Excellent

Figure 1 *Market research is all around you.*

When your next holiday brochure appears there is a line stating '100% of our customers rated their holiday excellent or above!' Beware of the obvious dangers.

In this book we will show you how to plan research, collect data, select samples and analyse and present the results of your research.

A successful musician needs to rehearse, a successful team player needs to practise and a successful business needs to research. You will need to be well organised: keep notes of all your sources, plan your work and keep back-up copies of everything. Don't learn the hard way!

Good luck and enjoy researching!

| Marketing research

Introduction

For a business to become and stay successful it must:

- find and keep customers, who may be consumers or other businesses
- understand and keep ahead of its competitors
- communicate effectively with customers to satisfy their expectations
- react quickly to changes in market conditions.

To do this it will need to research its market for information.

Have you ever been stopped in the street or telephoned by someone saying that they are doing market research? The people who are asking the questions are market research interviewers, working for a market research company. Market research is concerned with finding out about or investigating a market, e.g. why do customers buy existing products? Would they buy a new product?

> **Note!**
> The Market Research Society has over 8,000 members in 50 countries.

Marketing/market research

The Chartered Institute of Marketing (CIOM) has defined marketing research as 'The objective gathering, recording and analysing of all facts about problems relating to the transfer and sales of goods and services from producer to consumer or user'. For example, this means obtaining data to identify customers' needs and wants, or spotting market opportunities, analysing them and then using the information to reduce the risk when making marketing decisions.

So the essential components are:

> Market research is the home-work that needs to be done before a successful marketing decision can be made.

Inputs	Process	Output
Gathering data and fact finding	Analysis	Decisions and controls

Marketing research is concerned with the whole range of marketing activities; it includes all aspects of the four 'Ps' which make up the marketing mix, competitor research, business/economic research and forecasts.

> **Key term**
>
> **Marketing mix** – the ways in which the four 'Ps' (price, product, promotion and place) can be used by the company to influence consumers.

> **Note!**
> Both consumers and businesses can be surveyed in marketing research.

As a result of the Data Protection Act 1998 (DP Act) the Market Research Society has produced the following definition of classic survey (or market) research:

'The application of scientific research methods to obtain objective information on people's attitudes and behaviour based usually on representative samples of the relevant populations. The process guarantees the confidentiality of personal information in such a way that the data can only be used for research purposes.'

Source: www.marketresearch.org.uk

 Data Protection Act, page 83

Market research forms part of marketing research and is concerned with the investigation of consumer needs and preferences to find out the potential size of the market for a particular product or brand. It can be carried out by any organisation at every stage of the product life cycle, e.g. when developing or launching a new product, to increase sales or to extend the life of the product.

What is included in marketing research?

Here are some examples of research that could be carried out. If you check out the websites of any marketing research company you will find many more, (try surfing under marketing research companies, then go to products or research solutions).

- **Nature of the market**: for example, the size of the market by volume or value, potential for future sales, analysis of trends, estimates and forecasts of market share, profiles of the market segment, e.g. the characteristics of the target population – lifestyle, interests, income, etc. (market research).
- **Product research**: organisations will want to find out if there is a gap in their product range, how this could be filled and whether there is a market for a new product. They may need to assess the impact of packaging and how well it stands out on supermarket shelves. They could compare their products with those of competitors to investigate buying habits, or investigate the best advertising media to use.
- **Competitor research**: for example, who are they, whether they have similar products and what their prices are, how well they perform, how they will react to a new product/competitor, what their customers think, their strengths and weaknesses.

> Each week Asda researches the prices of 1,350 lines of northern and southern stores of Kwik Save, Safeway, Sainsbury, Somerfield, Tesco, Morrison, Iceland and Superdrug.
>
> Source: Competition Commission

- **Price research**: this could include calculating the elasticity of demand for products, collecting data on competitor prices, assessing how customers view prices and whether a price change would be acceptable, e.g. what would be the maximum price consumers would be willing to pay, how to price a new product – very low (penetration) or very high (skimming).
- **Promotion research**: includes measuring the effectiveness of advertising before and after an advertising campaign, the impact of promotion on demand, using population data and targeting market segments to establish where to promote products, and looking at the effectiveness of aftersales service.

Key term

Product life cycle – a model of the possible life of a product through launch, growth, maturity, saturation and possible decline. Not applicable to all products.

Note!

If you think market research is expensive try making a major marketing decision without it.

You can find out about competitors' products by using trade directories, telephone directories, web searches and personal observation. See: www.marketresearch.org.uk; MrWeb.

If you want a job in market research check out the careers section of company websites.

Key term

Elasticity of demand – the responsiveness of demand to changes in price.

 Targeting market segments, page 8

3

- **Place or distribution research**: includes the effectiveness of different outlets and channels of distribution, the suitability of new locations based on demographic and customer segment data, or the effectiveness of different supply arrangements.

Role and purpose of market/marketing research

Every organisation will have its own reasons for carrying out marketing research but essentially it is about collecting and analysing market data to satisfy customer needs, e.g. by adapting current products or developing new ones. It can do the following:

1 **Reduce the risk of business failure**: any business that produces goods or services does so at a risk. Research can reduce the risks and increase the chances of success. When the Mars Bar was relaunched in March 2002 with the slogan 'Pleasure you can't measure', the launch came after an intense period of marketing research prompted by a fall in sales from £2b in 2000 to £1.1b in 2001. Mariah Carey was dropped by EMI at a cost of £30m after her album failed in the market. How much marketing research do you think EMI carried out? Good research will identify possible risks and reduce the level of uncertainty involved in decision making.

2 **Improve decision making at the strategic and operational levels of the business**: for example, investigating attitudes and monitoring usage such as the age profile of users, how much and how often they purchase (which can affect pack size and stock levels), their views and opinions (see Table 2).

'Usage and Attitude' (UA) studies are complex, large scale and expensive; however, smaller surveys can be carried out.

Note!

The Ansoff Matrix is a technique for making decisions about new products/markets.

Table 2 Decision making at the strategic and operational levels

	Marketing research needed
Strategic decisions e.g. changing the direction of the business	• Market forecasts, trends and share • Competitor intelligence • Corporate image • Gap analysis – are there products missing (the gap) from the current range? Are there new markets that could be exploited? (Ansoff Matrix)
Operational decisions	Effectiveness of current price, promotion, product and place policies

3 **Forecast future trends in order to anticipate customer needs**: the business will need quantitative estimates of future sales and potential sales over a range of prices; it wants factual data and numbers of people. This information can then be compared with the cost of achieving the extra sales revenue.

4 **Define markets and identify buying habits**: this will help the business to pinpoint its target market and meet their needs precisely.

Communication with the customer can then be customised for each group, e.g. business or leisure travellers on the same flight.

5 **Inform proactive planning in the marketplace**: a business needs to develop new products to keep ahead of its competitors. In a Unilever Annual Report, the Chief Executive of Unilever said, 'We define the need, create the brand. Innovation is moving so fast that you need to be scouting ahead and creating markets'. Unilever is using its market research in the same way as Nokia – 'we are leading the consumer forwards' – continuously researching the market. Both these companies use research to be proactive, i.e. to lead the marketplace rather than follow. Did you know that you needed 'new Persil Colour Care' or a new ring tone?

Researching customers

To meet its customers' needs and therefore improve its chances of survival a business will need to know:

- how many customers there are
- how much they are willing to pay, including their buying habits and patterns of spending
- what their needs, desires, expectations, likes and dislikes, attitudes and prejudices are
- how it can best inform, persuade and convince customers to purchase the product
- what motivates customers and what attracts them to particular brands; for example, it could be the quality, design, colour, safety, or guarantees given with the product.

Whatever decision is finally taken the business must be certain that its decision is based on accurate and reliable marketing research.

Quantitative and qualitative research

- **Quantitative research** uses large samples to find out, for example, the number and type of people who use or might use a particular product. It answers the question of how many people buy the product. The characteristics of buyers are quantified numerically. Results could show the percentage or proportion of people in particular categories, which is 'hard' factual information. Quantitative research is the most common method of presenting information to help with decision making. For example, 62% of customers said they preferred the 'own-label brand'.

- **Qualitative research** is carried out to collect 'soft' information such as the attitudes and perceptions of people, i.e. why people buy or do not buy a product, or what they think about the product. Generally, this information is collected using small samples so that people can be interviewed in depth.

> **Note!**
>
> In general, quantitative research uses closed questions, whereas qualitative research uses open questions (see page 26).

Table 3 shows some examples:

Table 3 *Examples of quantitative and qualitative research*

Quantitative	Qualitative
19% of the resident population of Bromley are under 16, 22% are over 60	'I thought the name Mach 3 was better than Triad or Vector 3 because it showed speed'
(Source: `www.statistics.gov`)	(Source: Gillette Focus Group)

ⒸASE STUDY

'Get Fleeced'

Shikako and Bryan are opening a new sports shop in their local area. The new shop will be called 'Get Fleeced'. They intend initially to stock a range of sports clothing and footwear. The area has a mix of residential neighbourhoods and the high street is an Acorn Type 19: 'Young Professional Singles and Couples'. They have found out who their competitors are (First Sport, JD Sports and Foot Locker) and also that Uniglo, a Japanese company selling fashionable sports clothing, has just opened in a nearby town. They know that you are doing a market research course and will be asking your advice at various times. (This will be a good opportunity for you to develop your skills in a real situation.)

The first questions that Shikako and Bryan have are given in the Activity below.

ⒶCTIVITY

Tasks

The following questions relate to the case study above. Can you answer Shikako and Bryan's questions for them?

1   What might be the role and purpose of market research in our small local business? What data should we collect?
2   What is the difference between marketing and market research? Which could we use?
3   What do we need to know about our possible customers?
4   Explain the difference between quantitative and qualitative research and say when each should be used.

CASE STUDY

Market segmentation

Have you been to the music festivals at Brighton or Glastonbury, or the Proms?

The music industry is an excellent example of how segmentation works in marketing, recording, performance, distribution, broadcasting, etc. The music industry is segmented in many ways: age, price, singles and albums market, genre and so on. Genre can be further split up into pop, rock, classical, dance, etc. Dance can be divided further, e.g. house, garage and trance, and these can be subdivided further into 'niche' or smaller segment markets (see Table 4):

Table 4 *Segmentation within the music market*

House	Garage	Trance
Hard	UK	(Please complete yourself)
Euphoric	2 Step	
Progressive	US	
Latino		

Latino can be found at the Pacha Club in London.

Figure 2 *Lunchtime atop a skysraper, New York, 1932*

The top recording companies such as EMI, Sony, Universal and BMG have separate labels, which concentrate on different genre, e.g. EMI has a dance label Positiva, which includes artists like Spiller (Groove Jet), and Universal has Def Jam (Hip Hop). The young are targeted by pricecutting the singles (e.g. Westlife) to drive them up the charts. The European Union is now looking at ways of cutting prices to reduce illegal web copying.

With kind permission of P and CJ Lewis

CTIVITY

Tasks

The following questions refer to the case study on page 7.

1 Why does the industry break down its market into smaller and smaller segments? What does it hope to achieve?

2 Which segment are you in? Would anyone know? Do you spend money on CDs and albums?

3 Could you segment the other music genre?

I Market segmentation

Businesses try to split whole markets into smaller units or segments so that they can focus their marketing and other activities at specific groups of people. A market segment is a group of homogeneous or similar customers characterised by age, income, geographical area (local, regional or national) and/or lifestyle (e.g. taste in music). This is demonstrated by the products people buy. For example, the car market can be split into economy, family, sports cars, etc.

This extract from a press release (for white chocolate) shows how Nestlé uses segmentation.

> 'The advertising strategy aims to establish the brand positioning as playful, carefree spontaneity. The target audience is all chocolate lovers – primarily women aged 20–35, but not excluding men. The core age will be 25 years old.'

Banks target 18-year-olds at the beginning of the new academic year. How? Where? A large food manufacturer could target supermarkets.

Note!

Both consumers and businesses can be targeted in market segmentation.

ACORN

Acorn stands for Alternative Classification of Residential Neighbourhoods (see Table 5). It is available through CACI Market Analysis Limited. Here is a simple way to find out the lifestyle characteristics of your postcode area:

- Go to Multimap.com.
- Put in your postcode and a map will be displayed.
- Below the map click on 'Up my street'.
- Enter your postcode again.
- Click on ACORN profile (under local information).

An entry would show demographics or age profile, socio-economic profile (level of education, type of employment) attitudes, housing, ownership of durables, leisure, food and drink.

Here is an example of the amount of detail you can find:

ACORN Type 30

'The striking thing about this ACORN Type's usage of packaged goods is the enormous amount of dog food purchased, more than double the average.'

What could you do with this information?

Source: CACI

A CTIVITY

1 Find the full ACORN profile for your postcode and look at each heading. Do you recognise yourself or your household?
2 If you were going to market a new product in your area what would you choose? Would a new sports shop succeed? Justify your choice.

Table 5 *The Acorn Profile*

	Group		Type	% of GB population
Group 1	Wealthy Achievers, Suburban Areas	Type 1	Wealthy Suburbs, Large Detached Houses	3.0%
		Type 2	Villages with Wealthy Commuters	2.7%
		Type 3	Mature Affluent Home Owning Areas	2.8%
		Type 4	Affluent Suburbs, Older Families	3.8%
		Type 5	Mature, Well-Off Suburbs	2.7%
Group 2	Affluent Grays, Rural Communities	Type 6	Agricultural Villages, Home Based Workers	1.5%
		Type 7	Holiday Retreats, Older People, Home Based Workers	0.6%
Group 3	Prosperous Pensioners, Retirement Areas	Type 8	Home Owning Areas, Well-Off Older Residents	1.4%
		Type 9	Private Flats, Elderly People	1.1%
Group 4	Affluent Executives, Family Areas	Type 10	Affluent Working Families with Mortgages	2.8%
		Type 11	Affluent Working Couples With Mortgages, New Homes	1.15
		Type 12	Transient Workforces, Living at their Place Of Work	0.4%
Group 5	Well-Off Workers, Family Areas	Type 13	Home Owning Family Areas	2.1%
		Type 14	Home Owning Family Areas, Older Children	3.2%
		Type 15	Families with Mortgages, Younger Children	2.0%
Group 6	Affluent Urbanites, Town and City Areas	Type 16	Well-Off Town & City Areas	1.2%
		Type 17	Flats & Mortgages, Singles & Young Working Couples	0.9%
		Type 18	Furnished Flats and Bedsits, Younger Single People	0.4%
Group 7	Prosperous Professionals, Metropolitan Areas	Type 19	Apartments, Young Professional Singles and Couples	1.0%
		Type 20	Gentrified Multi-Ethnic Areas	1.0%
Group 8	Better-Off Executives, Inner City Areas	Type 21	Prosperous Enclaves, Highly Qualified Executives	0.8%
		Type 22	Academic Centres, Students & Young Professionals	0.7%
		Type 23	Affluent City Centre Areas, Tenements and Flats	0.9%
		Type 24	Partially Gentrified Multi-Ethnic Areas	0.7%
		Type 25	Converted Flats and Bedsits, Single People	0.9%
Group 9	Comfortable Middle Agers, Mature Home Owning Areas	Type 26	Mature Established Home Owning Areas	3.0%
		Type 27	Rural Areas, Mixed Occupations	3.4%
		Type 28	Established Home Owning Areas	4.4%
		Type 29	Home Owning Areas, Council Tenants, Retired People	2.3%
Group 10	Skilled Workers, Home Owning Areas	Type 30	Established Home Owning Areas, Skilled Workers	4.1%
		Type 31	Home Owners in Older Properties, Younger Workers	4.0%
		Type 32	Home Owning Areas with Skilled Workers	4.7%
Group 11	New Home Owners, Mature Communities	Type 33	Council Areas, Some New Home Owners	2.8%
		Type 34	Mature Home Owning Areas, Skilled Workers	2.6%
		Type 35	Low Rise Estates, Older Workers, New Home Owners	2.7%
Group 12	White Collar Workers, Better-Off Multi-Ethnic Areas	Type 36	Home Owning Multi-Ethnic Areas, Young Families	0.9%
		Type 37	Multi-Occupied Town Centres, Mixed Occupations	1.8%
		Type 38	Multi-Ethnic Areas, White Collar Workers	1.3%
Group 13	Older People, Less Prosperous Areas	Type 39	Home Owners, Small Council Flats, Single Pensioners	1.9%
		Type 40	Council Areas, Older People, Health Problems	1.3%
Group 14	Council Estate Residents, Better-Off Homes	Type 41	Better-Off Council Areas, New Home Owners	2.6%
		Type 42	Council Areas, Young Families, Some New Home Owners	2.7%
		Type 43	Council Areas, Young Families, Many Lone Parents	1.7%
		Type 44	Multi-Occupied Terraces, Multi-Ethnic Areas	0.8%
		Type 45	Low Rise Council Housing, Less Well-Off Families	2.0%
		Type 46	Council Areas, Residents with Health Problems	1.5%
Group 15	Council Estate Residents, High Unemployment	Type 47	Estates with High Unemployment	0.9%
		Type 48	Council Flats, Elderly People, Health Problems	0.9%
		Type 49	Council Flats, Very High Unemployment, Singles	1.1%
Group 16	Council Estate Residents, Greatest Hardship	Type 50	Council Areas, High Unemployment, Lone Parents	1.8%
		Type 51	Council Flats, Greatest Hardship, Many Lone Parents	0.7%
Group 17	People in Multi-Ethnic, Low-Income Areas	Type 52	Multi-Ethnic, Large Families, Overcrowding	0.5%
		Type 53	Multi-Ethnic, Severe Unemployment, Lone Parents	1.1%
		Type 54	Multi-Ethnic, High Unemployment, Overcrowding	0.5%

Reproduced with the permission of CACI Market Analysis Ltd

Figure 3 Strong marketing brands

 ACORN pages 8–9

Types of market segmentation

Markets can be split into segments in many ways, the particular choice will depend on the type of company, the characteristics of the market and the type of product.

Geographical segmentation

Here the market is split into homogeneous/similar groups on the basis of where people live or customers are located, e.g. countries, regions, counties, cities, urban or rural. An organisation can then target its marketing mix at a particular group. Proctor & Gamble, for example, produces and markets different flavours of Pringles in different countries to suit local tastes; salt & vinegar flavour allegedly does not appear in Belgium.

Coca-Cola (Figure 3) has deliberately pursued a policy of marketing the identical product worldwide (although it is researching the possibility of introducing Vanilla flavour cola for the US market), whereas Nokia has differentiated its mobile phones for different markets.

Source: Coca-Cola UK website

Geo-demographical segmentation

This is an extension of geographical segmentation which also includes housing, attitudes, a socio-economic profile, ownership of consumer durables, leisure activities, food and drink. One of the best known geo-demographical approaches to segmentation is ACORN.

Demographical segmentation

This uses variables such as gender, age, income, size and type of household, occupation, ethnicity, religion and family type, etc. to segment the market. This is quantitative data. Market research needs to be used to identify each segment.

- **Age**: particularly important and many companies now produce and sell to specific age groups, e.g. children's toys and clothing manufacturers use gender and a 1–2 year age range such as 'suitable for 3 to 5 year olds'. Baby foods have 3 metres of shelf space at supermarkets. Older drivers get cheaper car insurance, students pay more! 'We only insure careful drivers,' says one company, which presumably means that other companies only insure more risky drivers with consequently higher rates! Any complaints?
- **Gender**: many products are gender specific, such as health and beauty products or magazines; however, effective market research has shown a need for male fragrances and cars designed specifically for women drivers. Can you give some other examples?
- **Family type**: very often research is carried out with groups that represent the main stages in the family life cycle. This enables the survey to be representative of a wide variety of ages and lifestyles. Here is an example of groupings from the Advertising Standards Association survey, 'The public's perception of advertising in today's society':

- Teenagers 16/17/18 still at school.
- Singles aged 20–24.
- Parents with at least one child aged 5–14.
- Empty nesters aged 50–60 (children have left home!).
- The greys aged 65–75.

Reproduced with permission from the
Advertising Standards Association

A group particularly sought after are the DINKies, or 'dual income no kids'. Why do you think this is the case?

 **CTIVITY**

Tasks

1 How does your school or college segment its students?
2 How does your local leisure centre segment its customers? (Look at types of membership and pricing structure.)

Psychographic and lifestyle segmentation

Lifestyle is our way of life as reflected in our activities, interests, habits, opinions and friends. We show it in what we wear, the food we eat, the music we like. These all have implications for consumer spending. The analysis works on the assumption that people in a particular segment will have similar attitudes, desires, expectations and buying habits. Marketing campaigns can then be created which specifically appeal to their motivations. To work effectively the target segment must be measurable, substantial, accessible and be able and willing to buy the product. A number of classifications exist, many of which have been proposed by market research companies, e.g. AC Nielsen, Young & Rubicam and Taylor Nelson Sofres.

C **ASE STUDY**

How long have you had your mobile phone?

This research, carried out by TNS (www.tnsofres.com) looks at mobile phone ownership over the 12 months to April 2002. It reveals that age is a significant factor in the length of time that consumers keep a handset. Consumers aged between 12 and 24 have had their phones for an average of 17 months, whilst 35–44-year-olds have had theirs for an average of 21 months.

There are six million pre-pay handsets, purchased in the six months before Christmas 2000, which are still in use. These are coming up to the 20-month mark so users may be looking to change their handsets. In order for mobile phone manufacturers and network providers to market their products effectively, it is vital that they understand their target consumer groups. Overall, the research discovered that people are beginning to hold on to their phones for longer.

Source: Taylor Nelson Sofres

ACTIVITY

1 The data in the case study above is secondary data. Carry out a small class survey to see how you compare. For example, have you changed your mobile phone more or less often?
2 Why do you think older people keep their phones for longer?
3 What implication does the research have for:
   a retailers
   b manufacturers?
4 What target group are you in?

Behavioural segmentation

This type of segmentation splits the market according to consumer behaviour such as attitudes towards the product, buying habits, loyalty, usage and most importantly the benefits gained. This process examines the benefits that people hope to gain when they buy a product, e.g. do you buy toothpaste to clean your teeth or to give you 'fresh breath confidence'. (Colgate used this research to create the advertising slogan 'The Ring of Confidence'.) Why do you use perfume or aftershave? Does the 'born on …' (date) on Budweiser (the baby beer) '… sold a month later' attract you, did you know about this, do you care? Why do you buy it? Perhaps you want to win one of the 20,000 prizes. What benefits do you expect from a product such as a mobile phone? Research shows fashion to be important. Does it matter to you?

Usage refers to the status of the user, e.g. first-time user, non-user, heavy user, occasional user, ex-user, etc. Identifying the category of user enables the business to create a marketing mix to target each segment; essentially the objective is to convert non-users into users, and occasional users into regular users.

Tasks

1 How would you categorise yourself as a user of these products: Coca-Cola, Colgate toothpaste, Nokia mobile phones, Walker's crisps, your local leisure centre?
2 Could you be tempted away from your favourite brand? What would it take?

We are familiar with the concept of **loyalty** through the use of loyalty cards (see Figure 4) – stores try to keep customers returning by offering e.g. air miles, vouchers, discounts, etc. Loyalty can be classified on a scale of total loyalty to no loyalty. Much advertising is designed to create brand loyalty, particularly when the product is cheap and competition is fierce.

Figure 4 An example of a loyalty card

Tasks

1 Do you always buy the same brand or buy from the same shop?
2 Do you occasionally buy other brands?
3 Do you always switch brands, i.e. show little or no loyalty?
4 Would a loyalty card make you change your habits?

> **Note!**
>
> There are over 11 million active users on the Nectar card database. Boots claims 14 million on its Advantage Card.

The conversion model

This model looks at users and non-users of a brand (see Table 6). It examines consumer loyalty or how much people are committed to the brand, i.e. the likelihood of a repurchase by users or a first time purchase by non-users.

Table 6 The conversion model of usage

Users (of McDonalds)

Committed		Uncommitted: what would a competitor need to do to get you to switch?	
Entrenched	Average	Shallow	Convertible

Non-users (of McDonalds)

Available: what would a competitor need to do to get you to switch?		Unavailable	
Available	Ambivalent	Weakly	Strongly

Here are some definitions of the terms.

- **Entrenched** – the majority of your spending goes on the same brand (i.e. you **always** go to McDonalds!).
- **Shallow** – you may not repurchase, you may spend more on other brands, e.g. Burger King.
- **Convertible** – you are least likely to repurchase. What would it take to get you to go to Burger King – a special offer, two for the price of one?
- **Available** – you are the most likely to switch to McDonalds.
- **Strongly unavailable** – you are least likely to switch (i.e. you always go to Burger King!).

With thanks to `www.conversionmodel.com,` *accessed through* `tnsofres.com.`

 CTIVITY

Give examples of brand loyalty from your own experience and enter them on the chart. For example, do you always go to McDonalds, or do you sometimes frequent Burger King, KFC or Pizza Hut?

How can this information be used?

The conversion model forms the basis of many surveys on brand usage and loyalty. It is a particularly helpful approach for a new business hoping to break into an existing market.

1 New brands may be developed (new outlets opened) if numbers of uncommitted and available consumers are high.
2 Finding out how many consumers are committed to the product or are unlikely to repurchase allows the business to create a marketing mix directed specifically at those about to switch out of/into the brand.

> **McDonalds plans to sell 135 outlets. Drageo is trying to sell Burger King (2002).**

 CTIVITY

Trevor, Richard, Ivor & May (TRIM) wish to open a sandwich bar on the local high street. There are several local competitors. How could they use the conversion model approach to research the market? How could they segment their market?

Conditions needed for successful segmentation

For market segmentation to work effectively four conditions need to be present:

1 **Measurability:** it must be possible to measure the size of the segment using both the number of potential buyers and the amount

> **Key term**
>
> **Segmentation** involves dividing a market into smaller groups of consumers, each of which should be influenced by/respond to a different marketing mix.

they are willing to spend. This will enable the organisation to plan its provision. For example, the size of a segment can be found under ACORN types (`Multimap.com`), Keynote/Mintel for national figures, Neighbourhood Statistics (`www.statistics.gov`).

2 **Substantiality**: the market segment must be large enough (by value or volume) to make targeting the market worthwhile. Ideally there should be prospects for growth.

3 **Accessibility**: for example there may be barriers to entering the market such as a lack of the necessary start-up finance; perhaps a high level of advertising is needed to change customer perceptions; entry may be controlled by law, e.g. mobile phone companies had to bid for a limited number of digital licences. Organisations must be able to promote, deliver and distribute to the market, i.e. create a marketing mix that makes entering the market cost-effective and profitable; the organisation must be capable of meeting the needs of the segment. The costs of entry must be less than the expected returns.

4 **Uniqueness**: each segment should have specific needs and characteristics. These could be geo-demographic, psychographic or behavioural. For example, in one ACORN classification 75% more people than average shop daily for their groceries yet on average they purchase fewer fresh foods than other groups. This uniqueness is important as it enables retailers to specially create a marketing mix directly targeted at that segment. Supermarkets would avoid this area because people do not buy in large quantities. However, corner shops do well.

> **Niche markets**
> A niche market is a relatively small, clearly identifiable, self-contained segment within a larger market.
>
> With **high-value products** the number of customers can be very small, e.g. the Rolls-Royce Corniche (only 250 were 'hand-crafted' in 2000; see Figure 5) and the Park Ward (only 200 will ever be built). Only 525 Rolls-Royce Camargues were built between 1975 and 1986 at Willsden in North London.

Figure 5 A car niche market!

How can segmentation analysis be used?

Once the segments have been identified through research, an organisation will be able to:

- create a marketing mix for each group based on the research that it has done
- carry out further sampling using the segmentation
- analyse and profile customers, e.g. by age, income, consumer spending, financial status, etc., which can help with decisions about where to open new stores (for example, WHSmith used this to identify new retail sites)

- create a database structured by segments to help with marketing, e.g. the Co-op
- develop demand and market potential forecasts, e.g. Cellnet
- stock those goods that potential customers have identified.

Table 7 *Benefits and problems of segmentation*

Benefits of good segmentation	Problems with poor segmentation
Helps with:	
• marketing planning, different plans for each segment	• wrong sample size or sample frame, leading to invalid or unreliable data
• creating a marketing mix for each segment	• segments may be missed
• identifying gaps in the market	• inappropriate targeting or marketing strategy
• identifying and targeting specific groups	• missed opportunities for developing new products
• future research, e.g. quota or stratified sampling (pages 44–47)	**Note:** poor segmentation may occur because the four conditions are not present.
• choosing the best type of research, e.g. personal contact for businesses, focus groups for qualitative research	

Tasks

I As part of your preparation for this unit you will probably be required to carry out some form of market research. Once you have decided what to do, begin by segmenting the market you are going to investigate.

2 What four conditions need to be present for segmentation to work successfully? Are these conditions present in your market?

Tasks

Read through the case study on page 6 again. Here are some more questions from Shikako and Bryan.

1 Can you explain each type of segmentation and why we should use it?

2 Which type of segmentation is most suitable for a sports shop?

3 How could we measure the size of a local segment?

Planning market research

The planning process involves answering six questions:

1 What/who needs to be surveyed to get the answers we need?
2 Who should we ask?
3 How should the survey be carried out?
4 When should the survey be carried out to avoid bias?
5 Will the results be sufficient to solve the original problem?
6 What constraints might we face?

These questions can be set out as a series of steps required to carry out a market research survey.

Step 1: Set objectives

The first task is to isolate and define the issues, e.g. a poor level of sales to a particular age group; it is then possible to fix the boundaries or limits for the research. Always try to narrow the problem down to make it easier to investigate. Objectives should be SMART to enable the final results to be evaluated more easily. SMART is an acronym for:

- **Specific**, e.g. for a particular product or area
- **Measurable**, such as a percentage change in sales or profit
- **Attainable** or **achievable**
- **Relevant** or **realistic**
- **Time constrained**, i.e. within a set time period or deadline.

> ### BT Plays SMART
> BT has its sights on increasing Broadband connections to the Internet. Currently (2002) there are 150,000 connections in the UK. BT has set its objective as 1m by the year 2003 and 5m by 2006 with a 6–8% annual growth in revenues. (Reported in *Sunday Business* April 2002.) BT says these objectives are 'tough but achievable'.

The Market Research Society (www.marketresearch.org.uk) in its Code of Practice says that objectives should be clearly set with the researcher at the beginning of any survey to avoid conflict and misunderstanding later on.

For example, what sample size is needed, what is the deadline, how much will it cost, what data is expected?

> **The objectives of 'Get Fleeced' are to identify the brands/items of sports clothing and footwear it should stock.**

Step 2: Identify the target population

A successful business will need to know who its consumers are, what are their needs, how well these are being satisfied and what more it can do so they remain committed to the business. Markets can be segmented using several methods. Market research works on the basis that there are identifiable groups of consumers who behave in roughly the same way; these are the **target segments** – the people who need to be reached. These can then be sampled to gain an overall view of the population. Finally, these market segments may be targeted with a customer-designed marketing mix.

Market segmentation, page 10

Note!

The key to successful research is to do all the ground work before the research is carried out.

What is included in a research proposal?
- Introduction/background
- Timing
- Sample size
- Sampling frame
- Methodology
- Questionnaire structure and design
- Project management
- Costs

Step 3: Identify sources and availability of information

The first source of information for any business should be its own internal records. If this does not prove sufficient information then the business should look at the external data that has been published (remember this will also be available to the competition). Only if these two cheaper sources do not work should an omnibus survey, i.e. sharing a survey with other companies to cut costs, be considered (see Figure 6). The most expensive option for the business is to use a market research agency or conduct its own survey.

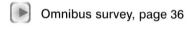
Omnibus survey, page 36

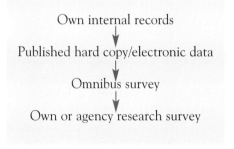

Figure 6 *Sources of information for a business*

The availability of information must be established before any primary research is carried out to avoid any unnecessary expense.

Step 4: Decide on the sampling frame

This is the group from which the sample will be selected. It would be determined by the objectives of the survey and the preliminary research.

It may cover several segments or just one, e.g. mothers with new born babies. If a list of items already exists then the researcher can proceed with a full random sample. The members of the sampling frame must be those which the business is trying to reach with its marketing.

> **How a business can create its own sampling frame**
> On the application form for the Boots Advantage Card, it asks 'If you have any children under the age of sixteen what are their dates of birth?' and 'If you are pregnant when is your baby due?'

Step 5: Choose the sample and the sampling method

The choice of sample is important. A wrong choice can distort results and give a false impression of the population. The sample must give valid and reliable results that can be used to predict how the target population will behave under similar conditions to the survey. Many sampling methods are available to the researcher. The choice would depend on the availability of a sample frame, whether a rigorous scientific result is needed or an approximation is acceptable, and the accessibility of the sample and cost, which depends on the complexity and size of the survey.

 Sampling methods, pages 43–48

Step 6: Decide and design the method of research

The plan should include: the sources and availability of internal/external secondary data, the level and accuracy of the response, e.g. whether personal contact is needed, and any deadlines that need to be achieved.

 Methods of research, pages 24 and 49

> **Validity and reliability of data**
> **Validity**, relates to whether your questionnaire does what it is supposed to do. Would a different group of people give different answers, possibly leading to a different strategy? Would the same group of people give the same answers if you tried again?
>
> **Reliability** relates to whether the questionnaire consistently gives the same answers each time it is used; that is, can it be depended on?

Step 7: Review costs and construct a budget

This depends upon whether the company is using an outside market research company (in which case it needs to consider how much it is willing to pay for the research) or is carrying out the research itself. In the latter case the budget plan should include an estimate of all likely costs that may be incurred. These will depend on the size of the sample, the expected response, the number of people involved, the time and deadlines, the degree of accuracy and reliability and whether the survey will be local, national or international. Generally, the more complex and difficult the survey, the more expensive it will be, e.g. interviewing a specific market segment would cost more than a mainstream survey. Greater accuracy, reliability and shorter deadlines only come at a higher price.

Here are some examples of current pricing: 'prices for a 90-minute group with a reasonably straightforward sample (mainstream lager drinkers, mothers who buy cereals) with summary report range from £1,850 to £2,200, and a one-hour in-depth interview ranges from £500 to £650'. (Tim Porter, AQR Library, Counting the Cost, www.aqr.org.)

Step 8: Estimate and set timings to cover times, dates, resources and locations

For this step it is best to use a Gantt chart or action plan. Set the deadline for the completion of the total project, include specific time for analysing and presenting the results. Fix the days and times for your research, these are important.

Figure 7 *'Feeling Guilty? Take a bunch home!'*

ⒸASE STUDY

ABC is considering whether it is worthwhile opening a small tobacconist/newsagents shop in the local station. It carries out a survey of passengers (the potential customers) every morning between 10 a.m. and 12 noon for a week. The results show that there are very few people using the station and ABC decides not to go ahead with its plans.

The CBS survey on the other hand, is carried out between 6.30 a.m. and 7.00 p.m. for a week. It discovers a large potential demand between 7.00 a.m. and 9.30 a.m. from the AB social group going to work; from 3.30 p.m. to 4.30 p.m. with the local secondary school pupils going home and from 4.30 p.m. to 7.00 p.m. with people returning home. It decides that there is sufficient business to open for two hours in the morning and three hours in the evening. The shop is now thriving and also sells flowers on Friday with a notice that reads 'Feeling Guilty? Take a bunch home' (see Figure 7).

ⒶCTIVITY

Tasks

1 Assess the strengths and weaknesses of each approach described in the case study above.

2 How would a plan have helped ABC?

A **Gantt chart** identifies and sets out deadlines for each activity in a project. The Gantt chart in Table 8 sets out possible activities for a market research project. Here the deadline is in Week 9.

Table 8 Gantt chart of possible activities for a market research project

Activity	Week 1	Week 2	Week 3	Week 4	Week 5	Week 6	Week 7	Week 8	Week 9
Start project, establish scope of the research and budget									
Set SMART objectives									
Carry out preliminary research									
Identify market segments									
Construct and test questionnaire									
Verify sample frame and select sample method									
Select research method, carry out research									
Data returned, coded and analysed									
Data presented, close project									

 **CTIVITY**

Construct a Gantt chart similar to the one above to plan your own market research project.

Step 9: Carry out the research

Whenever research is carried out the researcher must always act legally and professionally. Here are some of the 'Guidelines for research among children and young people' published by the Market Research Society. The main aims are to:

 MRS guidelines, page 84

- protect the rights of children and young people physically, mentally, ethically and emotionally and to ensure they are not exploited
- protect the researcher and client (children are those under 16, young people are aged 16 and 17).

Consent must be obtained

Consent of a parent or responsible adult should be obtained for interviews with children under 16. Consent must be obtained under the following circumstances:

- in home/at home (face-to-face and telephone interviewing)
- group discussions/in-depth interviews
- where interviewer and child are alone together.

When research takes place in schools the right of individual children/young people to opt out must be stressed by the interviewer:

- research must not encourage illegal behaviour such as underage drinking or gambling.
- research should only be conducted in a safe environment.

Tasks

1 Why do you think the guidelines described above are necessary for both the interviewer and the interviewee?
2 How will you ensure that you follow them?

Step 10: Evaluate the results

Have objectives been achieved? Are the results reliable and valid? To make sure that they are, quality control checks must be built into the survey process at all stages.

Questionnaire design

Do the questions work, i.e. collect the data they are supposed to? Do they cover all relevant market segments? Do they satisfy the survey objectives? Every questionnaire must be piloted/pre-tested.

Piloting

Certain circumstances demand particularly rigorous piloting. For example:

- when dealing with unfamiliar concepts – observation (watching pilot interviews) or qualitative pilots, can help to ask questions in the right way
- where it is obvious that the interview is potentially very complex or lengthy
- where questions could cause offence
- when it is necessary to review and test alternative question strategies.

Source: Market Research Society

Sample methodology and the collection of data

Has data been properly collected according to the original specification, e.g interviewing the correct quota. Field interviewers need to be effectively supervised.

 Quota sampling, page 47

Results

Has the data been honestly and fairly analysed and presented?

Step 11: Analyse the results

This step needs to be built in to the survey from the beginning. How will the results be achieved? Can the data be easily summarised/totalled? A range of statistical techniques will need to be used to obtain an overall view of the data, e.g. averages.

CACI PayCheck

Mean, median & mode income

What is it? CACI is a large marketing firm that provides companies with information to help them market their products more effectively. One of its services is called PayCheck, which provides information on people's income throughout the UK. PayCheck is made up of three databases, one of which is called 'mean, median and mode income'. This can give the average family income for any area in the UK, whether it is an individual postcode, or a wider area. It can be used for mailing lists (sample selection) or to improve customer databases where income data is missing.

Source: www.caci.co.uk
This site also has an excellent overview of the ACORN system.

 Mean,median and mode, page 62

 ACORN system, pages 8–9

Step 12: Present the results

The requirements for this step must be agreed with the client at the beginning of the project. For example, is a full face-to-face presentation required in addition to a written report? Does the client want decisions and recommendations on the survey topic or just the raw data? Are they prepared for an unpleasant set of results, e.g. being told 'yes, your sales have risen by 20%, but the market as a whole has risen by 200% so that compared to your major competitor you are much worse off'?

When forecasts go wrong! The Darth Vadar fiasco

When the fourth Star Wars film was released, Dorling Kindersley predicted a huge demand for merchandise. It printed 13m Star Wars books, yet only 3m were sold. DK profits fell and it was taken over.

I Primary research methods

What is primary research?

This is research carried out for the first time to collect first-hand or primary data. The data is collected and used for a specific purpose. The data will be original and up to date. It can be obtained either by the company's own research, e.g. original sales invoices or it could be collected by a market research agency on behalf of the company, e.g. surveys carried out in the street. Primary data can be expensive to collect but it will be exclusive to the company, it is not available to competitors.

The choice of method will be determined by many factors, for example if a wide area has to be covered it may be more appropriate to use postal questionnaires because these can be cheaper than using interviewers. When the type of information required is complex or difficult, trained interviewers could give a better result. In practice it is a matter of balancing the cost and effort involved against the rate of response. Higher response rates are usually more expensive to obtain because they require more personal contact.

Researchers use various methods to collect data. A major way of collecting primary data is to use questionnaires.

Questionnaires

A questionnaire is a set of printed questions that is given to a specified number of people to collect statistical data. It can be completed by the respondent (the person answering the questionnaire – self completion) or the interviewer can write down/input the answers which the respondent gives. The principle applies whether the questionnaire is given face-to-face, by telephone or online.

Using the Internet

Pop Up Questionnaires are becoming a regular feature of many Internet sites. The advantages for the companies distributing these online questionnaires are lower costs (as no interviewers or mailing are needed), higher speed and the ability to survey a larger number of more willing people (because people have visited a website freely). Any company with a website should be able to survey its customers online. The disadvantages could be that the company doesn't really know about the people replying. Does Colonise really want to know the views of a UK resident in an unknown segment?

Customers may well become irritated with seeing a questionnaire every time they visit. Questionnaires must be simple and capable of self-completion (see Figure 8). Current thinking suggests that online questionnaires should be seen as an additional way of surveying customers rather than the only way, e.g. in a recent survey BT gave respondents the choice of either an online or a hard copy response.

Congratulations

Receive a special $115 thank you package when you take Colonize's 5-second survey.

Please help us by answering the following three questions.

1. Over the past 3 months, how many movies have you seen in the theater?

| Please Pick ▼ |

2. During 2002, how will your spending habits compare to last year?

| Please Pick ▼ |

3. How many leisure trips do you plan to take in 2002?

| Please Pick ▼ |

Thank you! Where should we send your thank you package?

Your email: [   ] Submit

(You must be at least 13 years old to participate.)

Thank you for your participation. We'll send our thank you package composed of over $115 worth of special offers. You'll also receive our exclusive special offer emails. Sponsored by Colonize.

Figure 8 On-line questionnaires must be simple and capable of self-completion

Before a questionnaire is written the researcher must:
- obtain as much information as possible about the research topic to be able to construct the questionnaire, e.g. through discussion with the client, library/Internet research, etc.; this will enable the researcher to identify the market segments
- have a clear goal and precise SMART objectives
- have an idea of the type of data results that are needed and expected, e.g. quantitative or qualitative, whether they are likely to be favourable or unfavourable and how they could be analysed and presented
- make provision for pre-testing or piloting the questionnaire to sort out problems before the questionnaire goes live
- decide how it will be distributed and returned, e.g. a heavy bulky questionnaire can be expensive to send and have returned by post; generally the higher the level of personal contact the higher the level of response; however, it is more expensive

We used **Keynote** and **Mintel** reports, *Social Trends* and the *General Household Survey* to find the information we needed to construct our questionnaire.
The main objective of the questionnaire is to find out which brands/items of clothing and footwear to stock.

- make arrangements for non-response and call back if telephone interviews are to be held
- have a back-up list of possible respondents in case any of those originally chosen drop out
- have a clear idea of the resources and budget available.

Computer-assisted Telephone Interviewing (CATI)

The telephone interviewer uses a computer and a computer-designed questionnaire. The respondents' answers are directly keyed in using a code. The computer is programmed to carry out the analysis of the data automatically, and results are available almost immediately.

The purpose of a questionnaire can be:

- to gather general information about the respondent, such as age and occupation – this will later be used to determine/confirm which market segment or category people belong to
- to collect the specific data required for the investigation – whenever possible a trial or pilot survey should be carried out first to ensure that the final questionnaire works and will achieve its purpose.

Types of questions

A number of techniques may be used to construct a questionnaire:

- **Dichotomous questions** – these are close-ended/closed questions with only two possible choices, for example, yes or no; agree or disagree; true or false. They are good for providing quantitative information.
- **Multiple choice** – these are also closed because a definite answer has to be given. However, in this case there are more than two choices.
- **Open-ended/open questions** – these do not have a predetermined answer. They are often used by retailers to find out customers' opinions. Although they are good for gathering qualitative information, they can be difficult to interpret. For example, 'How were you treated by the sales people?' could produce the reply 'Very nicely'. But what does 'nicely' mean?
- **Scaled or rated questions** (also called **semantic differential questions**) – these give the respondent a fixed range of possible replies (see Figure 9). For example: 'I would now like you to give your opinion of how you would expect AA staff to deal with breakdowns. Below is a list of comments that have been made about AA staff. First of all please give your opinion of the service you would expect from AA telephone staff in the event of a breakdown. Please show your answer by ticking the relevant box using the scale 1 to 10 shown below, where 10 is the most positive answer and 1 is the most negative answer.'

	10	9	8	7	6	5	4	3	2	1	
H. Efficient	☐	☐	☐	☐	☐	☐	☐	☐	☐	☐	Efficient
I. Courteous/polite	☐	☐	☐	☐	☐	☐	☐	☐	☐	☐	Rude/abusive
J. Helpful	☐	☐	☐	☐	☐	☐	☐	☐	☐	☐	Unhelpful
K. Professional	☐	☐	☐	☐	☐	☐	☐	☐	☐	☐	Unprofessional
L. Warm/friendly	☐	☐	☐	☐	☐	☐	☐	☐	☐	☐	Cold/unfriendly
M. Respectful	☐	☐	☐	☐	☐	☐	☐	☐	☐	☐	Patronising/condescending
N. Reassuring/calming	☐	☐	☐	☐	☐	☐	☐	☐	☐	☐	Brisk/abrupt
O. Concerned/interested	☐	☐	☐	☐	☐	☐	☐	☐	☐	☐	Unconcerned/disinterested

Figure 9 Example showing scaled (rated) questions (with thanks to the AA)

Some basic rules on how to construct a questionnaire

1 Give an explanation of the questionnaire at the beginning. For example, here is the switchboard introduction for a readership survey for the *Times Educational Supplement* carried out by the Croydon Market Research Centre.

'Good morning (afternoon, evening). I'm from Croydon Market Research Centre. We're conducting a study among educational establishments throughout the UK. In order to ensure that we interview a random cross-section of teachers I would like to speak to a teacher whose surname begins with the letter (A–Z). As a way of saying thank you for participating we will be making a donation of £2 to the UNICEF Afghan Appeal on behalf of each person who takes part in this survey. The interview should take about 15 minutes. As members of the Market Research Society we are bound by a Code of Conduct, which ensures strict confidentiality for all your answers.'

2 Every question should be essential. Beware of the temptation to ask too many questions.

3 Questions must not be ambiguous. There must be only one interpretation possible.

4 It should be easy for people to understand the question. For example, 'Do you walk to school?' is better than 'Do you perambulate to school?'

5 Every question should be precise because vague questions will only confuse people.

6 Questions must not be biased or break the equal opportunities laws. An 'ethnic monitoring' question can be asked, when the respondent decides the group to which he or she belongs, e.g. 'Which of the following groups do you belong to?'

7 Questions should be short, because asking and answering questions costs time and money. Always say how long the interview is likely to take.

8 Questions should not embarrass people by being too personal or complicated. What sort of question would embarrass you?

9 Questions should be carefully laid out using lots of space.

10 Questions should be arranged in a logical order and follow on naturally.

 Code of conduct, page 84

11 Wherever possible provide 'tick boxes' or a rating system to allow people to answer quickly and easily, for example, the answer to the question 'What is your attendance on this market research course?' could be rated as: Excellent, Very good, Satisfactory, Fair, Poor, Don't know, or Don't care.

12 All questions and answers should be coded to allow for simple computer input. The results and analysis of the data could then be done quickly if the CATI system is being used.

13 Remember to say 'thank you' at the end of the questionnaire.

Reproduced with permission from Croydon Market Research Centre

 CATI, page 26

Self-completion questionnaires

These are questionnaires that can be filled in by the respondents themselves without the need for a trained interviewer. They should be self-explanatory with only simple guidance necessary so no further interviewer support is needed. They can be distributed through newspapers, e.g. The Business Readership Survey; by post, e.g. the Consumer Panel Survey, and returned by Freepost, i.e. reply-paid envelopes, or in person, as with Census forms.

Questionnaires can be used by any business:
- a local corner shop
- a charity that wants to know if its members are satisfied
- the Greater London Authority (GLA) researching residents' views on mayoral priorities for London
- BT's 'Have your say in shaping BT services and help ChildLine', available online and as a self-completion postal questionnaire (23 closed questions and 2 open-ended questions, e.g. What improvements could be made to the service? (The customer account number would totally identify every respondent.)
- Williams Press surveying its business customers.

ⒸASE STUDY

'Get Fleeced'

Questionnaire

'Get Fleeced' is opening a new sports shop in the area. To help us provide you with the best service possible we would be grateful if you could take about five minutes to complete this questionnaire. Any information you provide is strictly confidential.

1 Do you take part in any sports?

Yes ☐ No ☐

If No go to Q3.

2 Which of these sports do you play?

Keeping fit	☐	Swimming	☐
Walking	☐	Racket sports	☐
Team sports	☐	Golf	☐
Indoor games	☐	Other	☐

Other sports please say ....

3 How old are you? Please tick

15–24	☐	25–34	☐
35–44	☐	45–54	☐
55–64	☐	65+	☐

4 Which of these brands have you bought during the last year?

Nike	☐	Adidas	☐	Reebok	☐
Ellesse	☐	Timberland	☐	Other	☐

5 Which of these sports items are you most likely to purchase in the next three months?

Fleece	☐	Tracksuit	☐	Waterproofs	☐
T shirts	☐	Football kit	☐	Swimwear	☐
Golf clubs	☐	Tennis kit	☐	Footwear	☐

6 When you visit a sports shop, which of the following do you think is important? Please tick.

	Extremely important			Not at all important	
	1	2	3	4	5
Variety					
Low prices					
Value for money					
Quality					
Changing rooms					
Service					
Good displays					
Own label goods					
Range of brands					

7 How much do you normally spend when you visit a sports shop?

Under £20 ☐	£21–40 ☐	£41–60 ☐		
£61–80 ☐	£81–£100 ☐	£101+ ☐		

8 We intend to offer a range of extra services. How important do you rate each of these? Please tick the box.

	First choice			Last choice
	1	2	3	4
Hire of equipment				
Testing equipment before purchase				
Restringing tennis rackets				
Selling sports tickets				

9 Where do you usually shop for sports clothing and footwear and why?

....

....

10 Do you ever watch football on TV?

Yes ☐ No ☐

11 Do you agree that a new sports shop would be a good idea?

Yes ☐ No ☐

Figure 10 Questionnaire for "Get Fleeced"

Table 9 Notes on the construction of the questionnaire

Questions	Comments
1	Used to gain attention. Interview could be closed, but many sports items are bought for fashion. A routine statement is included: this is automatic with computer-assisted systems.
2	The categories are based on preliminary research using the Keynote Report 'UK Sports Market'.
3	The age groups are those in the Target Group Index (TGI) used in most commercial reports. Data collected here can be compared with much larger samples.
4 & 5	These will get the data needed to make business decisions.
6	A 'scaled' or rated question, 1/2 or 4/5 answers will help decision making. The categories will be based on preliminary research.
7	The categories are based on the type of product/outlet.

8	Designed to get specific information.
9	An open-ended question.
10	Why is it here?
11	A leading question using 'agree' tends to get agreement: is this fair?

ACTIVITY

The following questions are based on the 'Get Fleeced' case study above.

1 What type of question is question 1?
2 Why has it been put first?
3 What could happen to the interview if the respondent says 'No'?
4 How does 'Close interview' help the interviewer/interviewee?
5 What is missing from question 6? Are all factors considered?
6 Can you say why the answers to question 8 will help the business decide which extra services the shop should provide?
7 Question 9 is an open question: state two reasons why this type of question has been used. Do you think it is an effective way to collect this information?
8 How might question 10 help the business, if at all?
9 Which questions will produce quantitative data and which will produce qualitative data?
10 Question 11 would sometimes be called a 'leading' question. What does this mean?
11 Why do you think that categories were used in question 2 instead of a list of all sports?
12 How has the sports market been segmented in the questionnaire? Say why the method/s have been chosen.
13 Assess whether this questionnaire meets the rules suggested on page 27.
14 Will this questionnaire meet the objectives set by 'Get Fleeced' on page 25?

ACTIVITY

The principal of your college/school has asked your group to carry out a market research survey to find out what students think of the institution and its courses.

Tasks

1 Construct a questionnaire that covers college/school facilities, cleanliness, atmosphere, library, the quality of the courses, details of the respondent and suggestions for improvement. Test/pilot the questionnaire against the thirteen points before you carry out the survey.

 How to construct a questionnaire, pages 27–28

2   When you have decided on the sample carry out the survey; you can use whatever method you wish providing you give your reasons.

3   Analyse and present your results to your group.

Interviews: face-to-face and telephone

Types of interview

- **Structured interviews with closed questions**: this is a formal interview during which the interviewer will ask a set number of prepared questions usually based on a questionnaire. Most street interviews are structured. It is a face-to-face method of gathering data. For example, 'Do you like the new design? Please tick yes or no', is a closed question because there are only two possible choices.
- **Structured interview with open questions**: in this case instead of having to answer yes or no the respondent/interviewee can express a personal opinion. For example, 'What do you think about the new packaging?' is an open question and many answers are possible.
  - Open questions take much longer to answer because interviewees have to think about their reply, i.e. they do not have a pre-set choice of answers. This means that interviewers have to spend more time with each interviewee, which costs more.
  - Open questions are much more difficult to analyse, which also takes time and money. Open questions are used when the business wants the whole range of possible answers that may be given.
- **Semi-structured interview**: more informal, directed interview where the interviewer will try to guide the interviewee by prompting and asking follow-up questions that encourage replies, i.e. it is more flexible than the structured approach. It tends to be expensive because more time is involved, but a good response rate is expected.
- **Informal**: The interviewer is able to steer the discussion in any direction considered appropriate. The method is often used in surveys where an informal/in-depth approach is required.

 Focus group, page 36

ACTIVITY

Analyse the advantages and disadvantages of each type of interview. When should each be used?

Which interview to choose

The structured interview with closed questions is quick and easy to carry out and is the easiest to analyse; however, the respondent cannot give extra information. The informal methods take time and are difficult to analyse because of the wide variation of replies. The best approach for a simple survey is a structured approach with both closed and open questions (the majority should be closed to make analysis easier). It may be possible to code qualitative replies to questions such as: which features of the product do you consider most important? This can be done by giving a list of features such as quality, colour, design, etc.

CAPI: What happened to pen and paper?

The Taylor Nelson Sofres Consumer Omnibus surveys over 2000 adults every week by face-to-face interviews. Interviewers use CAPI (Computer-assisted Personal Interviewing) multimedia pen technology, which allows for faster inputting of answers as no 'pen and paper' are used. Companies can ask more complex questions, interviews flow better and costs are reduced because data entry, coding and checking are integrated. CAPI is particularly useful for large-scale continuous government and commercial surveys, such as the Labour Force Survey.

Source: Taylor Nelson Sofres

How to conduct a good street interview

- Dress smartly.
- Be polite, pleasant and speak clearly.
- Use positive body language.
- Choose a busy area.
- Do not be seen eating.
- Be well prepared.
- Keep safe.
- Find out if you need permission.
- Street and telephone interviewers must always identify who they are working for, and be prepared to give a contact telephone number.
- The company carrying out the research should ideally be registered with the Market Research Society and follow its guidelines.

When to close an interview

Closing an interview means to end or finish the interview. Look at this example taken from a questionnaire:

> Question: 'We are interested in your views on the content of the sport pages in *The Sun* newspaper … Do you read *The Sun*?
> 'Yes …' (continue interview)
> 'No …' (close interview).

The interview is closed because the interviewee does not read *The Sun* so cannot contribute to the survey. Only the views of readers of *The Sun* would be needed. Other reasons for closing an interview include:

- making sure that the right people are selected so the data are reliable and useful
- allowing interviewers to spend time with people needed for the research
- to avoid wasting the interviewees', interviewers', and clients' time and money.

A **field survey** or **field research** is any original primary research carried out by directly contacting or observing the respondents, e.g. at work, home, in the street or while shopping. Field research can include face-to-face interviews, observation, hall tests and opinion polls. The particular method chosen will depend on:

- the availability of existing internal/external information
- the deadline and the size of the sample
- the level of accuracy and the complexity of the survey
- the objectives of the survey – remember qualitative research might be useful for views and opinions, but are these reliable? It is not hard evidence or fact.

Postal survey

This is original research where questionnaires are posted to respondents for self completion. The questions need to be straightforward as there is no one to help or explain. Reply paid/freepost facilities will need to be provided to try and make sure that the questionnaires will be returned. There is a high level of non-response and companies sometimes make charitable donations for every questionnaire which is returned completed. Would you reply when there is no personal or real charitable incentive? The advantages are that costs can be budgeted, a wide area can be covered and a large number of questions can be asked because people have time to respond. (The Business Readership Survey distributed with the newspaper had sixteen A4 pages.) Postal surveys work best when the respondents have a direct interest or reason for completing them, e.g. cat owners being surveyed about a new cattery or members of a society being asked about services.

 CTIVITY

Would you advise 'Get Fleeced' to use a Postal Survey to research its market?

Continuous research/survey

This is research that is carried out on a regular, ongoing basis to provide data on trends, e.g. sales data by type of customer collected and analysed weekly can provide a time series, which is essential for analysing patterns and trends. Continuous research can be secondary or primary (which is more expensive). Here are some examples of ways in which continuous research can be carried out:

 Time series, page 68

- **Retail audits**: provide long-term information on how products sell in the shops, e.g size of the market, market shares of the leading brands categorised by region and type of store. Audits are carried out by market research companies and would be bought by a business every two months so that trends can be analysed.
- **Tracking studies**: are concerned with the long-term monitoring of consumer awareness of the brands in a specific market, e.g. brand name and advertising. They tend to be large scale and generally only cover well-known brands.
- **Consumer panels**: are set up on a semi-permanent basis. The members are chosen so that they represent the views of the population as a whole, i.e. they are supposed to be a cross-section. Unlike focus groups they do not meet together and there may be many hundreds of people involved. Panels usually report regularly to a marketing agency. They may be asked to report on price changes, package design, a new ingredient, etc.
- **Electronic monitoring**: electronic point-of-sale (EPOS) equipment, which reads the bar code on products as they pass through the checkout, allows almost every business to track its sales and stock movements and monitor customer reactions to special offers, etc. If the customer has a loyalty card the business will also be able to build up a complete database of customer purchases. Do you have store or loyalty cards? Are you worried about the amount of information the store has on you?

> **Note!**
>
> Retail audits, tracking studies and consumer panels are unlikely to be used by a small business.

Would you expect 'Get Fleeced' to use any of these methods of continuous research? If not, which companies are most likely to use it?

Ad hoc, custom-designed and omnibus research

Ad hoc or one-off market research – this is usually carried out to meet a specific need on a particular occasion. Many *ad hoc* surveys are custom designed. They can be expensive to design, plan and implement unless opportunities are created to reuse materials, e.g. for a follow-up study.

Custom-designed/made-to-measure or tailor-made research – this is a specially created survey designed to find the answers to specific questions. Because it is unique it can be very expensive to design and collect; however, it should provide exact relevant data that will be exclusive to the business. Data collection may be done by the business or through a data collection market research company. Both large and small businesses use custom-designed research.

Omnibus research – a marketing research survey where several companies can contribute their own questions to a multipart questionnaire. It is ideal for those companies with a small number of questions that need answering. Costs can be shared between the participants. The main problem is getting the participants to agree their questions and their position on the questionnaire.

Source: Croydon Market Research

Focus groups

A focus group is a group of five to ten people – supposedly ordinary or representative consumers – brought together by a market research company in an informal environment to talk – in a directed way about a general subject such as tinned fruit, chocolate, TV programmes, sports shops, etc. It is in effect a collective interview. The main purpose is to get general views about the 'product' and to find out people's needs, desires, expectations, hopes, attitudes, fears and emotions. It is qualitative market research. Several sessions need to be run to give a fairer view of the population as a whole and make the results statistically reliable. They are best used at the beginning of a project when it is still possible to make changes to the product. Focus groups are usually put together by an agency on behalf of the organisation launching or changing a product.

They are used frequently because they are cheap and easy to set up and supposedly give the honest views of the person in the street. They give immediate feedback from a precisely targeted market segment. Problems can occur if the group is too large and splits up or is not managed effectively. It is important for the researcher to remain neutral and focussed and not steer the group, which could give a biased result, i.e. the group may be influenced by the researcher and not give honest replies.

The case study below begins to cast doubts on their reliability and validity.

> **Note!**
>
> Group interviews: the best known example of a group interview is the Focus Group.

 Focus group, page 32

CASE STUDY

Why we need more virgins

Policy decisions about everything from beans to banks are influenced by focus group findings. TV producers reshape programmes, brands are repositioned, new products are launched or abandoned, employees are hired or fired and ultimately companies survive or fail.

This makes it essential for the qualitative research industry to be reliable. There is growing alarm over focus group recruits. The same faces are showing up evening after evening. It is as if a new breed of regulars is attending focus groups – the word 'stooges' comes to mind – with growing expertise in what the researcher wants.

This is all a far cry from the innocence, openness and spontaneity marketers may expect from such sessions. As David

Dimbleby said, 'The BBC has lost the knack of quick decision making because it relies on endless focus groups and analysis'. Virgins are people who are attending a focus group session for the first time.

Source: Marketing Business

ACTIVITY

1 Have you any reason to think that females and males would behave differently in a focus group situation? How might the outcome of the group be affected?
2 Which would be the best primary research method for a small retailer to use to obtain customers' views on the level of service? Give reasons for your choice.
3 Which would be the best method for a large, nationwide mail order company to use? Give reasons for your choice.
4 An existing company is intending to develop a new range of garden equipment: why would it find focus groups helpful?
5 'Get Fleeced' is considering whether to use telephone interviews or face-to-face personal interviews to get information about its possible customers. Which would you recommend and why?

Test marketing

This is the last stage of the market research process where products are tested in the marketplace. It includes hall tests, home tests, observation, pilot trials and test town operations or field trials.

In business it is often the case that companies do not have sufficient time or money to perform rigorous statistical analysis. Therefore, before a product is launched nationally manufacturers will often first test the reaction of consumers in a specific region. This may well include a full press and TV campaign with promotional back-up, such as point-of-sale advertising. For example, the launch of Guinness's Draught Bitter in cans involved giving out free cans at London mainline railway stations and asking for reactions.

The data that a company obtains in this way will enable it to decide whether it is worthwhile to go for a total nation-wide launch. The test area should ideally be a small version of the nation as a whole, i.e. with a range of ages, income, ethnic groups, lifestyles, etc.

BT tests out promotions in any one of nine regional zones to find out how well they work. 'By careful monitoring of what happens we can make adjustments to the product, the make up of our target group, the message of our advertising or whatever, then comes national roll-out.'

Source: BT

Hall tests

The public are invited into a local hall and asked to taste, smell ('sniff') or try out a product, the method is used to get qualitative data on the product, i.e. views and opinions. Products may have identical packaging or perhaps none at all so that people do not know which product they are testing; this is called a **blind placement test**.

Home testing
Products are placed in a sample of homes to find out how well or badly they perform in real use, e.g. Persil Liquid Capsules – 'Just put two in the drum and turn it on'. The users are asked to comment either by interview or questionnaire.

Observation
This is often carried out by store managers who watch/observe how customers react to new products or changes in store layout. Small businesses can observe reactions to shop window advertising. A non-participant researcher does not communicate but only watches behaviour, whereas a participant observer may join in and possibly influence events.

Pilot trials
Before new products are introduced into the market they are usually tried out on a very small number of people to find out what changes need to be made before any further money is spent on development. Many products get no further than this stage. A careful sample will need to be chosen – what appeals to one group may not appeal to another! The main purpose of a pilot is to identify and sort out potential problems.

Questionnaires are always piloted to find out if questions are valid and reliable, that is, do they test or find out what is intended.

Field trial or test town operation
This is a miniature version of a test market in which a product whose qualities have already been verified through blind placement tests (for example, asking consumers if they prefer A or B without the consumer knowing which is the new product, often carried out as hall tests) is marketed in a limited way so that actual movement through the shops can be audited. Consumers may also be asked to return pre-paid cards giving their views on the product.

Interpreting the results: the results from these cards would not be read as if they were representative of all consumers in the test town – the target population – but rather as an indication to be used to form a judgement. Therefore, if a few hundred returned cards show a consistent result, this would be sufficient justification to proceed with a wider launch. It is all a question of reconciling what is required with what is practical.

Great care needs to be exercised when interpreting the results of a test market operation, in case they are biased. In the Guinness example the following questions, among others, should be considered:
- Was the weather very hot?
- Was the competition advertising or reducing its prices? Both of these would influence the results of a field trial.

> The Pepsi Challenge and Daz Challenge (see Figure 11) were examples of blind placement tests; people were asked to compare two similar products and say which one they preferred. The challenges were run by Pepsi and Daz – Pepsi and Daz both came out best!

Figure 11 The Daz Challenge – a blind placement test

Whatever decision a company makes as a result of market research it should only do what it believes is right.

Table 10 Advantages and disadvantages of primary research methods

Method	Advantages	Disadvantages
Telephone interview (see Figure 12) – a structured set of questions is recommended	Easy to carry out, fast and convenient, flexible, satisfactory response rate; people may be more willing to respond over the phone	Can be expensive, depends on time and distance; respondents have little time to answer; body language cannot be seen; can be biased
Face-to-face interview – a personal interview between the respondent and interviewer	High response rate; flexible and easily controlled; extra questions can be asked; answers can be clarified; body language can be seen	Very expensive; needs trained interviewers; can take considerable time; can be biased unless people are carefully selected
Focus group	Can be used for in-depth investigation with immediate reaction and feedback	May attract the same group of people who give answers they think the researcher wants
Panel	Can cover a wide geographical area and cover a variety of topics	Panel members need to be rotated to prevent set answers being given
Observation – direct observation of a task or activity	Very accurate and can be easily controlled, e.g. accompanied shopping to find out what and how consumers buy; new businesses can observe competitors	Can be very expensive and time-consuming when full co-operation is needed from the people being observed
Postal surveys – for a postal survey a clear, questionnaire is needed	Costs can be controlled; people have time to respond; any area can be covered; people may be more truthful, particularly if the reply is anonymous	Very low response rate, i.e. the number of replies; questions cannot be explained or answers verified

Figure 12 *People may be more willing to respond over the phone*

Table 10 *(continued)*

Pilots & field trials	Can prevent costly mistakes later, relatively cheap and convenient; can test a range of features; immediate feedback	Results can be biased if the area is not chosen carefully
Omnibus research	A small number of questions can be asked relatively cheaply as companies can join a multipart questionnaire	Poor response rates with the postal version; there may be problems with defining the target market for all participants
Continuous research	Useful for analysing trends and changes as a bank of data can be built up	Continuous expense means that new and small businesses are unlikely to be able to afford it

 CTIVITY

1 Discuss the main methods 'Get Fleeced' could use to research the market for a new sports shop in your area. Which two methods would be most suitable?
2 Which methods would you not suggest and why?
3 How could 'Get Fleeced' use observation to research the market?

Choosing a sample

Research techniques

You should now have an effective questionnaire which is right or fit for the purpose for which it is intended. It is now time to use it with the people or businesses that you are trying to reach with your research:

- What information do you need to obtain?
- Which people or businesses do you need to contact?
- Where can you find them?
- Which is the best way of getting the information? Will a postal questionnaire be acceptable or are in-depth interviews needed? This depends on how much personal contact is needed with respondents.

The pilot testing of the questionnaire could have revealed which segments were missing or under/over represented and more importantly where they could be found. Do not be afraid to change your questionnaire at this point, or even start again. (But always remember that £000s are at stake!)

Note!

'Get Fleeced' has identified several sports clubs and a leisure centre that are possible target groups.

- Is a sample frame with a list of possible individual respondents available? If it is, you have no problems.
- Do you or the client know where to find them?
- If individuals cannot be identified, are there groups that could be contacted?

Sampling

Most market research surveys use samples to reach the people they need to contact. A sample survey is a systematic way of collecting primary information from a small part of the total number of individuals or items that could be investigated, for example, interviewing a small number of people in a shopping centre. The total is normally referred to as the population or universe, i.e all shoppers in the centre. For example, if Boots the optician was to carry out a customer satisfaction survey the population would all be people who have used the opticians; in a hairdressers it is every client. For industrial goods such as machinery the population is every business that has bought the machines. Remember that market research can involve other businesses as well as consumers.

The sample that is chosen should be representative, i.e. typical of the whole population. It is a cross section. The purpose of sampling is to find out and make estimates about the 'population', which are based on the results of the sample. Ideally a sample should be as large as possible and/or practicable, because a bigger sample will give more accurate results about the population.

The benefits of sampling a population compared to investigating every item – such as The Census of Population that counts everyone in the UK every 10 years (1991, 2001, 2011) – are that:

- the costs are lower
- inputting and analysis of the data is quicker
- greater flexibility and control are possible
- properly constructed, it allows the researcher to test out ideas about the population and find out the population parameters/limits, e.g. the average and dispersion of the data.

Bias in sampling

It is important that the sample represents the population. Bias refers to any influence which makes the results obtained from the sample differ significantly from the actual or true results for the population. Bias can occur because:

- the list of items from which the sample is selected is inaccurate or incomplete; for example, if the sample is chosen from the electoral register it must be up-to-date
- the sample is unrepresentative or untypical and does not cover the population, e.g. only interviewing people you like
- the sample is too small and cannot be used to predict the population

> **Key term**
>
> The **population** is the total number of items from which a sample is selected e.g. consumers or businesses.

> **'Get Fleeced' took great care to make sure that their questionnaire was pre-tested and all segments were represented to eliminate bias.**

- the selected people do not respond
- the interviewer introduces bias by leading the interviewee
- questions have been incorrectly constructed.

Tasks

1 What are the benefits of sampling?
2 Why might bias occur in a sample?
3 Why might these sample surveys be biased?
  - a survey intended to show the volume of traffic in your local area which is carried out between 10 a.m. and 11 a.m.
  - a survey intended to show the age of all shoppers at WHSmith carried out between 2 p.m. and 3 p.m.
  - a survey on the use of local entertainment facilities carried out between 9 p.m. and midnight on Saturday night.

> The sampling frame/database is very important and expensive information. The Readership Research Survey for *The Times Educational Supplement* used the database owned by the School Government Publishing Company. A survey of real ale drinkers would use as the 'population' members of CAMRA or the Campaign For Real Ale.

> Do you receive junk mail? How do they know who you are? Why do they think you will be interested?

The sampling frame

The sampling frame is the information required before a sample can be chosen. It is normally a list of all the items in the population to be sampled, for example, the electoral register or council tax list, all AVCE students, etc. Many market research companies now use postcodes (there are roughly 2,000,000 postcodes in the UK with an average of 15 addresses per postcode). Creating the database for a sampling frame can be a very expensive process, particularly if a very large number of items or individuals is involved, e.g. some 40 million people are on a database which shows their credit rating. Targeted lists of names and addresses can be bought from a company like 'Experian' for about £50 per thousand. The magazine *Marketing Week* usually has advertisements for companies selling such lists.

Where does all this information come from? Every time you fill in a form or respond to a phone-in you are providing information which will end up in a database and may be sold on.

Table 11 shows some examples of how you could be on a database – you can probably think of others. Are you concerned about the amount of information held on you?

Table 11 Ways in which you could appear on a database

Apply for car insurance	Phone in to vote for Big Brother	Buy £5 ticket to France in *The Sun*	Use a credit card or any other plastic card	Fill in an enrolment form for a course	Say you are 18 to become a member of a night club!	Buy a mobile phone or respond to junk e-mails

Types of sampling

Convenience sampling
The researcher chooses the most convenient or accessible people to interview for a survey, e.g. getting the views of football supporters outside the ground, street interviewers working near a busy bus stop. The method is often used in shopping centres when people have time to stop. Questions are usually designed to gather qualitative data, they are less reliable for quantitative data. Take care when interpreting the results of these samples, which are unlikely to be representative of the population as the method is not rigorous/scientific enough.

Judgement sampling
This is similar to convenience sampling, the interviewer selects people who in their judgement suit the survey; it is generally used in shopping centres or the street.

Random walk or location sampling
Random sampling: a random sample is one in which every item which can be chosen has an equal chance of being selected. For this to be achieved a complete sampling frame must exist with every item identified. Each item can be selected either by:
* sampling without replacement, which means that once an item has been chosen it cannot be chosen again, rather like numbers in the National Lottery
* sampling with replacement, which means that an item can be selected more than once.

There are several ways random sampling can be done. When the numbers are fairly small each individual can be allocated a number and the sample can be picked out of a box or hat, such as a raffle.

With random sampling, the selection of items should be unbiased and free from personal prejudice. Random sampling works better if the population or group is homogeneous or broadly similar; this means that any item that is chosen would be representative.

> **Note!**
>
> The CATI system is programmed to prevent the reoccurrence of numbers.

 CATI system, page 26

Key terms

Random samples – random sampling methods are systematic (random choice of first item), cluster (random choice of clusters), multi-stage (random choice at each stage), stratified (random choice within each strata).

Non-random samples – these are a quota sample including all items up to the quota allowed. Since random samples are more scientific they can be used for further statistical analysis.

CTIVITY

A retailer has carried out a sample survey of customers each Saturday afternoon for the past three weeks. The results of the sample do not reflect the sales of the shop for the whole week.

Task
Can you suggest what might be wrong with the sample survey, and how it could be improved?

Key term

Stratified sampling respondents are chosen from specific segments of the population.

Note!

The Office for National Statistics has brought out a new socio-economic classification, which will be used to classify people into strata.

Stratified sampling

A stratum (the singular of strata) is a segment or group of items with a set of common characteristics such as an income, social group or age. For example, teenagers aged 16–18 and singles aged 20–24 are two strata but so are 'department stores', 'supermarkets' and 'corner shops', which could be used in a market research survey of the sale of, for example, Pepsi. A stratified sample is one where items are specifically chosen from each stratum to represent the population. It can only be used when the population or universe can be divided into strata or groups. The members of each stratum will need to be known before the sample can be chosen.

Simple random sampling can then be used to select items, so that the sample should reflect or be representative of the whole population. A complete sampling frame is required and it must have enough information to distinguish between the strata.

Target Group Index (TGI)

Target Group Index (TGI) surveys use socio-economic groups to target people for research purposes, for example: Who reads *The Sun*? Who watches *Coronation Street*? The answers will determine what is advertised in *The Sun* and what adverts appear during *Coronation Street*. Although many characteristics can be used to classify people, occupation is most frequently used to indicate to which social class people belong (see Table 12).

Table 12 Target Group Index classification of socio-economic groups

Occupation	Social group	Social class
Professional managers	A	Upper middle
Middle managers	B	Middle class
Clerical/office	Cl	Lower middle class
Skilled manual	C2	Skilled working class
Manual	D	Working class
Students	E	

Look at any Keynote report to see how this is used.

 Keynote report, page 53

Generally, a stratified sample will give a more accurate picture of the population than a simple random sample, e.g. a group could first be divided into females and males to avoid only males or only females being selected.

CASE STUDY

Example of stratified sampling

Suppose a market research company is to carry out a survey of sales of cans of Pepsi sold in different types of retail outlet (see Table 13).

Table 13 Survey of sales of cans of Pepsi sold in different retail outlets

Strata retail outlets	X Population	Y Sample
Department stores	50	5
Supermarkets	80	8
Corner shops	150	15
Petrol stations	120	12
Total	400	40

Column X shows the number of retail outlets in each stratum. Column Y is the sample size required. The sample from each stratum is in proportion to the whole population of retail outlets.

The company usually samples 10 per cent. Therefore a total sample of 40 stores must be selected. For a representative sample 10 per cent of each stratum should be chosen: 10 per cent of supermarkets are required, therefore 10 per cent of 80 equals 8.

 **CTIVITY**

Read the case study above and then carry out the following tasks.

Tasks

1 What information will the market research company need before it carries out the survey?
2 What are the main advantages of a stratified sample compared with a random sample?
3 When should a stratified sample be used?

The government's statistical service uses stratified sampling to collect much of its information because it is cheaper and can give very reliable results. Table 14 is an example of the strata it works from to gather data about businesses. The 'chance of selection' refers to the likelihood or probability of a business being chosen and is the base for much of the government data.

Table 14 Stratified sampling

Employee numbers in strata business	Chance of selection
500 or more	Certain
200–499	1 in 2
100–199	1 in 12
50–99	1 in 16
11–49	1 in 48
10 and under	None

Figure 13 A small sample of our market research students

ⒶCTIVITY

Tasks

1 What method would you use to choose a sample of students to represent your group?
2 Give your reasons.

Key terms

Systematic sampling – the first item is chosen randomly and subsequent items are chosen at set intervals.

Multi-stage sampling – the population is subdivided into smaller and smaller groups and sampling takes place at each stage.

Take care! It is easy to miss the ninth person if the questionnaire is too long; perhaps every twentieth person would be better.

Systematic sampling

In this method the first item is selected at random. Subsequent items are then selected systematically; for example, every ninth item is chosen until the total number is achieved. The method is simple to organise and relatively cheap. It is most appropriate when the population/sampling frame is known to be broadly similar so that it does not matter which items are chosen or when the frame has been specially structured. A complete sampling frame is only required if a desk-based/computer-generated selection is to be made. In a street, however, every ninth person is relatively easy to choose.

Multi-stage sampling

This example shows how multi-stage sampling works:
A market research company has been asked to survey students in the European Union.
Stage 1 – choose a country. Each country would be given a number and then chosen at random. The sampling frame would be countries.
Stage 2 – the UK has been chosen, so the next stage is to assign numbers to counties and choose a county. The sampling frame is counties.

Stage 3 – your county has been selected. For this stage each school/college (the information needed for the sampling frame) would be assigned a number and one centre chosen by simple random sampling.
Stage 4 – your centre has been chosen. Market research students at the centre are now allocated numbers. A sampling frame of students is needed – for example, the register.
Stage 5 – you have been chosen to represent the views of students in Europe! Do you think you are representative?
This method avoids the need for a complete listing of all items, so a full sampling frame is not required, i.e. a list of all students in Europe is not needed. It is simple to organise and relatively cheap to implement because samples are taken in stages.

Cluster sampling

For this method to work the population should be composed of specific groups or clusters. A cluster could be a block of flats, all the sports shops in a sales district, or a specific postcode. Clusters are then chosen at random. Every item (e.g. person or shop) in the cluster is included in the sample. It is used when a complete sampling frame is not available, but a list of clusters is, or when the area to be covered is particularly large.

Cluster sampling is easy to carry out, providing the chosen items are close together, for example, housing estates or courses at a college. A team of researchers can be sent in to interview everyone, i.e. 100% of the cluster. The results could be biased if the chosen cluster is unrepresentative of the population so it is better to sample a large number of small clusters. Postcodes which usually consist of about fifteen houses have been classified into fifty two household clusters. Practically it is much simpler and cheaper to interview fifteen households close together than find and interview fifteen households randomly chosen across a wide geographical area.

> **Note!**
>
> Try to find places where people congregate or cluster together. Your sample may not represent the whole population but will be reliable for that group.

> 'Get Fleeced' have found a useful list of clusters including local tennis and football clubs, e.g. Petts Wood Reserves, winners of the Double 2001/2.

Quota sampling

Quota sampling is a non-random way of sampling. This means people are specially/deliberately selected because of their specific characteristics, e.g. a mother with a baby in a pram. It is often used by interviewers in the street, e.g. audience research surveys carried out on behalf of TV companies frequently use this method. For example an interviewer is given a total number of people to interview such as ten teenage girls and ten teenage boys; another researcher might have to interview twenty mothers with a child in a pram. Each interviewer has the responsibility of deciding who is to be included in the sample (see Figure 14); they will select and interview until their own quota is filled. Altogether the size of each quota should reflect the population in general. Therefore the sample should contain the same proportion of people with a particular characteristic as are found in the population. So if five per cent of the population are in the AB group, then five per cent of the sample should come from this group.

> **Key term**
>
> Quota sampling – sample items are chosen in the same proportion as they appear in the population.

Figure 14 Each interviewer is responsible for deciding who is to be included in the sample

 AB Group, page 44

Every interviewer has a quota or percentage to interview from each group. The system is cheap and convenient to carry out, no 'call back' is necessary as interviewers will work until the quota is achieved, but basic information about the population is needed. It is difficult to control as the choice of whom to interview is decided by the interviewers. How can you tell which group a person belongs to?

Table 16 Comparison of sampling techniques

	Advantages	Disadvantages
Convenience	Cheap & easy to carry out because the interviewer does not have to search/travel for respondents; useful 'qualitative' snapshot	Results can be unreliable as the choice of respondents depends on the interviewer
Judgement	As above	As above
Random	Rigorous; known chance of selection allows further analysis to be carried out; unbiased selection method	Expensive and time-consuming (travelling) if respondents are geographically spread out; a complete accurate/up-to-date sampling frame needed
Systematic	Random method; easy to administer in street interviews; does not need a detailed sampling frame	Call back is necessary when interviewing households, i.e. cannot substitute the home next door
Stratified	Sample should be more representative of the target population	Full details of the target population need to be known to create strata
Multi-stage	A complete sampling frame is not required; the last stage can be sampled randomly	It must be possible to identify stages at each level
Cluster	Samples clusters rather than individuals; little travel involved; whole cluster can be interviewed quickly	Needs a large number of small clusters
Quota	Quick, cheap and easy; low travel costs; no call back necessary	Subjective; based on researchers' opinions; non-random so less rigorous

CTIVITY

'Get Fleeced'

Tasks

1 The questionnaire has been constructed. Which method of collecting the data would you suggest? Look at the strengths and weaknesses of alternative methods and suggest the most appropriate.

2 What sampling method would you advise?

Secondary research methods

Secondary data is data that already exists, either published and available as hard copy/electronic sources outside (external to) the business or internally within the business. It has been collected by someone else for their own purpose. Secondary research investigates the sources of secondary data. It should be the starting point for all market research, however great care needs to be taken when using secondary sources and data. Always bear in mind that the data was not collected to answer your questions and this may have affected the data analysis and presentation (see Table 17).

When using data collected by someone else, the researcher should ask:

1 How much will it cost to obtain and use the data?
2 Which organisation collected the information?
3 Is the source reliable?
4 What purpose did the collectors wish to achieve? For example, statistics about smoking prepared by a tobacco company, or statistics about railway travel prepared by a road haulage pressure group are likely to be biased in their favour.
5 When were the figures collected? For example, yearly figures in the *Annual Abstract of Statistics* or *Social Trends* are not as up-to-date as figures in the *Monthly Digest of Statistics*.
6 What do they include/exclude?
7 What do the definitions mean?
8 Is the data accurate?

> **The first step in any research project is to find out what data already exists.**

> **Note!**
> Secondary research is also called **desk research**.

> **Note!**
> Always consider searching secondary data sources to be the first option.

Table 17 Using secondary data

Advantages	Disadvantages
• It can be a useful and effective substitute for expensive primary research	• It may not be fully relevant to the new users' needs
• Because data already exists, it can be relatively cheap to search	• It may be biased and unrepresentative; if possible look at a variety of secondary sources
• It can provide historical time series data for trend analysis	• Data may not be available for a particular topic or problem
• It can show the overall national or regional situation, e.g. 'How people travel to work' in *Social Trends* can be compared to a simple class survey	• It can be expensive to log on/register with specialist agencies for in-depth reports, e.g. Keynote
• It can be a good starting point for research	5 It could be out of date

Every business now has almost instant access to a vast amount of data via the Internet. Much of the general information is free, i.e it is available to you and your competitors, although more specialised sources can be expensive, especially for private subscribers.

Internal sources of secondary data: company records

This is data which already exists inside the organisation, perhaps on the company's own database or Intranet (see Figure 15).

Within the business, every department and section will have its own records which are a valuable source of market research data, e.g. in the finance department these are the invoices and customer accounts. The transport and stock departments could have records of stock movements, which show how quickly stock is sold, and distribution data which shows the outlets that perform the best. The sales department could have sales invoices and orders, sales figures and reports; there may even be existing market research reports which could be the basis of new research and enable the business to look at any changes which may have occurred. For example, the TES readership survey was originally carried out in 1996.

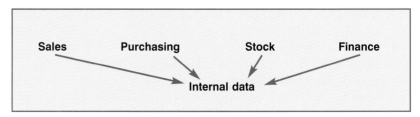

Figure 15 Internal sources of secondary data

All of this data could be used for market research into sales in specific areas. Although the primary use of these documents is in the original department, they become secondary data when used for market research, e.g. using invoices to investigate sales to particular consumer segments.

Internal sources should always be the first line of enquiry for any market research investigation because they should be cheap, fast, convenient and exclusive to the company, i.e. they are secret and not available to competitors. Especially important will be the availability of 'back data' or time series data which can be used for trend or time series analysis and forecasts (primary data, which is usually a snapshot of the current situation does not have this advantage). Beware of 'information overload', where too many statistics with too much unnecessary detail may be collected. Only if internal sources are unsuitable should the business move to external sources.

> ### Key term
> **Secondary data** – someone else's data being reused for another purpose, i.e. it is second hand.

CTIVITY

Tasks

1 Define secondary data and secondary research.
2 What internal secondary data does your centre or company have? Analyse its strengths and weaknesses. How could it be used for market research into possible new markets?

Which businesses could use secondary data?

Any business large or small could use external data but only existing businesses will have internal data. This may need to be reorganised and reanalysed before it can provide effective market research information, e.g. a newsagents could examine its customer postcodes (linked with ACORN) to stock new magazines.

 ACORN, page 8

External sources of secondary data

This is research carried out on data which is only available outside the organisation.

Government

There is a wealth of data available, which could help a business to:

- assess its market share, e.g. a business could compare its own sales with those of the total market by using the Government Product Sales and Trade series. (Aggregate or total figures are given so that individual businesses cannot be identified. If they could, then they would be unwilling to respond – why?)
- count the number of potential customers, their characteristics and regional distribution: e.g. 'Size Analysis of UK Businesses' gives details of retail shops and service establishments, The Census of

> *Loyalty cards*
> **Do you have a store card or loyalty card? Whenever you use a card in a store the details of every purchase you make are stored on a computer database. The information is used to give the customer points or vouchers, the store gets a complete record showing your name, address, average spend, reaction to advertising and special offers, etc – a very simple and effective way of gathering market research data!**

Population provides data on families and individuals (the results of the 2001 Census are now available).

Depending on the research needed the main written sources of external information published by the government are *Monthly Digest of Statistics, Annual Abstract of Statistics, Social Trends, Economic Trends, Regional Trends, Family Expenditure Survey, General Household Survey*. Most of these would be available in any reference library but a business could obtain the more specialist publications direct from the Office for National Statistics, which also publishes a free annual guide to sources of information. Much of this material is now available through the Internet at www.statistics.gov (particularly good for time series data with over 40,000 series available for viewing or free downloading, look at time series and datasets) and www.DTI.gov.uk.

Note!

Contact the Office for National Statistics at www.statistics.gov.uk

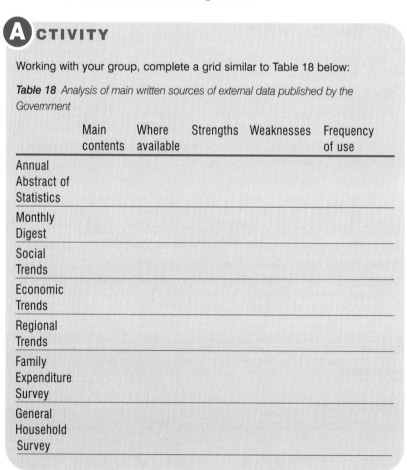

A CTIVITY

Working with your group, complete a grid similar to Table 18 below:

Table 18 *Analysis of main written sources of external data published by the Government*

	Main contents	Where available	Strengths	Weaknesses	Frequency of use
Annual Abstract of Statistics					
Monthly Digest					
Social Trends					
Economic Trends					
Regional Trends					
Family Expenditure Survey					
General Household Survey					

Computerised databases

Examples include ACORN (or the Alternative Classification of Residential Neighbourhoods) which can be accessed through www.multimap.com, www.dialog.com (lists of reports) and www.mrweb.com.

 Multimap, page 8

Commercial publications and Internet sites

The Internet can now be used to gather general information about almost any market, much of it is free although specialist commercial market research information is not normally available unless it is paid for, e.g. Keynote publications and Euromonitor reports are an excellent hard copy resource on a range of markets. They are available in most good reference libraries. Online at www.keynote.com only the summary reports are available to the casual user. Many market research companies provide useful information including case studies and survey methodology (how the survey is constructed and carried out). The Market Research Society (MRS) has a useful introduction to market research with a dictionary/glossary of terms and guidelines governing research.

Useful commercial Internet sites include www.keynote.com and www.euromonitor.com (with a wide range of product and sales data comparing the UK market with European markets). Mediavillage.co.uk is good for links to marketing and market research sites and includes RAJAR, which shows the audience figures for UK radio and BARB for TV audiences (the home page has the original 'Space Invaders' game!).

ACTIVITY

A local company is carrying out media research for a new advertising campaign. Check out the audience figures for your local commercial radio stations.

Information on a company and its competitors

This can be obtained by searching under the company name. This should reveal the product range, prices, special offers and current promotions. Using commercial companies which are expensive, you could 'legally and ethically' discover the launch date for a new product, enabling the client to run a major marketing campaign on the same day; anticipating competitor actions could help the client 'respond in advance of the event' (www.marketing-intelligence.co.uk/aware/case-studies). www.mrweb.com has hyperlinks to competitors in every sector. A simpler method suitable for small/start-up businesses is to check out the *Yellow Pages* or *Kelly's Directory* to find the names of competitors and then contact them pretending to be a customer.

Always name your sources – include the publication or website, table or reference number and date. This will help you and the reader to check the data. Keep a record of all sources – include a 'star' system to rate their usefulness/reliability. Always use the most up-to-date information. The 'Press Releases' section of sites, i.e. what the company has told the press, can be useful.

Note!

ESOMAR is the World Association of Opinion and Market Research Professionals, with over 4000 members in 100 countries. The website www.esomar.nl/ has guidelines covering a range of market research.

General publications, directories and other sources

These include *Kelly's Directory*, the *Yellow Pages, Yell.com,* and professional institutes such as the Chartered Institute of Marketing (CIM). Also the national press can be useful, e.g. *Financial Times* and *The Economist*, TEXTLINE, *Marketing Week, Campaign* (advertising).

Additionally, a wide range of information is provided by both national and international institutions, such as the World Bank, European Union (www.Eurostat.com), banks, trade unions, trade associations, the CBI and Chambers of Commerce. The local borough site usually includes a business section which is useful for research.

Table 19 Advantages and disadvantages of different sources of information

	Advantages	Disadvantages
Government	Reliable; cheap; easy to access; good for time series and initial searches	Could be too general to answer specific questions, e.g. data is national/regional; available to everyone
Commercial	Can answer specific questions; may be sector based; information only available to the researcher	Time needed to find a company; expensive
Competitors	Websites will show current position; free initial access	Information limited to what business wants to reveal; needs to be continuous to show trends
Retail audits	Current information about the market (in retail stores), size and market share, i.e. quantitative; can show trends	Need to be bought at frequent regular intervals; may not cover certain stores; little qualitative data
General publications	Up-to-date; easily available in most reference libraries; good for initial market research; online	Unlikely to answer specific questions

ACTIVITY

Tasks

1 With other members of your group, work together to create a database of websites that you have all used. Put in the exact address, which will allow you to connect directly with the site. Use a table similar to Table 20:

Table 20 *Database of websites used to gather information*

Address	Ease of use	Details of free information	Information used
www.statistics.gov			

2 a Give three advantages and three disadvantages of using secondary data.

b Why should a business look at secondary sources before starting primary research?

3 Joseph and Rose (JR) are looking at the possibility of starting a local laundry and ironing service. Initial secondary research on `www.statistics.gov` produced the information in Table 21 (clothing and laundry services):

Table 21 *Value of output of laundry services in the UK using different percentages of washload ironed: 2000*

Percentage of weekly washload	Total ironing (kg)	Value of ironing (£ million)	Total value of laundry services (£ million)
8	2,603	8,981	43,732
9	2,929	10,103	44,855
10	3,254	11,226	45,978
11	3,579	12,349	47,100
12	3,905	13,471	48,223
15	4,881	16,839	51,591
20	6,508	22,452	57,204

Source: HHSA estimates (totals rounded up)

'The largest proportion of time, 42 per cent of the total, was accounted for by ironing, with 39 per cent of time spent doing laundry – hand washing, loading and unloading the washing machine, hanging clothes out to dry and folding them (see Figure 16). A much smaller proportion of time was spent in making and mending clothes (19 per cent of the total). Females contributed a total of 85 per cent of the total time spent in laundry and clothing-related activities, with males contributing 15 per cent of the total. Females spent more than twice as much time on ironing than males spent in total on clothing-related activities.'

Source: UK 2000 Time Use Survey/HHSA estimates

Note!

1 billion =
a thousand million

Note!

HHSA stands for Household Satellite Account. It is produced by the Office for National Statistics. It measures and values the unpaid work carried out by households in the UK.

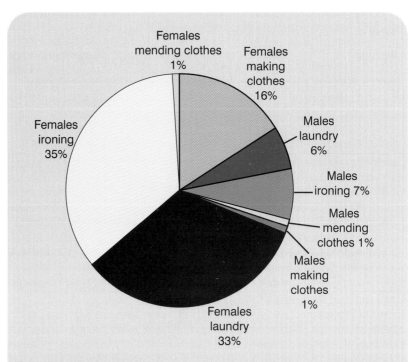

Figure 16 *Percentage of time spent by males and females on clothing-related activities: 2000*

Providing clothing and laundry services

'Laundry: Information on the average number of washing loads per week came from the Lever Faberge UK Laundry Market report. This was multiplied by the number of households in the UK (from the Family Expenditure Survey) to obtain the volume of washing. We obtained the weight of an average load of washing from the National Association of the Laundry Industry, and assumed that 10 per cent of each wash load is ironed. This is roughly equivalent to 5 garments per person per week.'

Value

'We used a launderette service wash price per load to value the output of washing, and an ironing price per kilo to value the output of ironing. A service wash includes drying and folding the clothes. Prices were collected by phone from a random selection of launderettes.'

(© Crown Copyright 2002, Office for National Statistics)

a What conclusions could JR draw from this information on the market potential and possible success of the business?
b What are the strengths and weaknesses of this information? What data is missing? What further secondary information might they need?
c What primary data might they want to collect? What methods should they use? Give your reasons.

Eventually JR will need to make a decision to start up or not. Market research can help but needs to be treated with caution. They will need to be totally convinced that the business will succeed. They should not let the market research get in the way of the right decision.

4 Comment on the strengths and weaknesses of the following secondary data from the point of view of a company intending to develop a sun cream aimed at males (see Table 22):

Table 22 *Attitudes to protecting self from sun exposure*, by gender, 1999*

Great Britain	Percentages	
	Males	Females
Very important	57	79
Fairly important	30	18
Not important	11	3
Don't know	1	–

* Among people aged 16 and over.

Source: Omnibus Survey, Office for National Statistics 2002

CASE STUDY

'Get Fleeced'

'Get Fleeced' consulted these organisations:
- their local borough council small business service
- Chamber of Commerce
- trade associations (see Figure 17).

They visited the local reference library to look at local trade directories to find out about the competition.

They used Keynote and Mintel reports to see national trends in the sector.

They found Tables 23 and 24 in Keynote reports on the UK sports market.

Figure 17 *Business Link is an example of an active trade association*

Table 23 Buyers of sports shoes by sex, age and social grade (%)

	1995	1998	2003
All adults	27	26	25
Men	34	32	32
Women	20	19	18
Age			
15–24	46	47	48
25–34	40	36	35
35–44	32	31	30
45–54	24	20	18
55–64	14	13	12
65+	5	6	6
Social grade			
AB	29	30	30
C1	29	27	26
C2	30	26	25
D	25	24	23
E	17	14	13

Source: Target Group Index, BMRB International, based on a Keynote report, 2003 (estimate based on industry sources)

Table 24 Estimated segmentation of the sports footwear market (£m and %)

	£m	%
Soft shoes (trainers)		
Running	125	9
Keep fit (indoor)	125	9
Racket sports	60	5
Football trainers, including 'black trainers'	60	5
High-sided, including basketball	50	4
General use [a]	380	29
Subtotal	?	?

Table 24 (cont.)

Boots/hard shoes [b]

Walking and climbing boots	125	9
Soccer and rugby boots	100	8
Skates (ice/roller/in-line)	50	4
Golf shoes	40	3
Other boots/technical footwear	185	15
Subtotal	?	?
Total	?	?

[a] Including cross-trainers and all children's trainers.

[b] Also known as 'brown shoes'.

Source: based on Keynote report

CTIVITY

The following tasks are based on the case study above.

Tasks

1 Calculate the subtotals and the totals.
2 Use the two tables to analyse the way the market for trainers has changed. Look at 'all adults' age and social grade.
3 How could 'Get Fleeced' use the tables to decide the items/brands it should stock?

Research analysis

The purpose of research analysis is to gain information about the population from which the sample was taken It involves a detailed study of the sample data. Analysis is usually done by the organisation that has paid for the market research although it can be done by the collector. At the end of this section you will be able to carry out techniques such as calculating percentages, averages and measures of dispersion, examining time series and forecasting, using market research data.

Data

Whenever someone fills in a questionnaire, answers a question or is observed as part of a survey, the results are called data. Raw data is data which has not been processed or altered in any way. Data has no real meaning – it may just be a page of numbers. It must be analysed and interpreted before it can provide information.

This is data: 6, 7, 9, 14, 26, 41. The fact that they are the winning numbers for the National Lottery is information.

Data > Analysis > Information

Averages (measures of central tendency)

When looking at the results of marketing research it is often useful to summarise the data. An average is a single figure that is used to give a general impression (summary) of the whole data. It is a representative or typical amount. Whenever an average is used extreme values tend to be ignored or their impact reduced; for this reason averages are sometimes called 'measures of central tendency'.

There are three types of average that can be calculated and used to analyse marketing data.

Mean

The most commonly used is the **arithmetic mean** or **mean**. This is calculated by:

$$\frac{\text{Total value of items}}{\text{Number of items}} = \text{arithmetic mean}$$

For example: What is the mean value of sales made by a shop over seven days?

Sales for 7 days =
£158 + £168 + £158 + £150 + £153 + £155 + £136 = £1078

$$\frac{\text{Total value of items (sales)}}{\text{Number of items (days)}} = \frac{£1078}{7} = £154$$

The arithmetic mean uses all the values and is only an approximation. £154 was not made on any day in that seven-day period.

Note!

The average family has 1.6 children!

A CTIVITY

Calculate the mean monthly spending on clothing by a sample of 'young fashionables' (see Table 25):

Table 25 *Mean monthly spending on clothing by 'young fashionables'*

1	£75	7	£87
2	£32	8	£140
3	£87	9	£78
4	£120	10	£87
5	£90	11	£101
6	£26		

Median

When all the values are placed in ascending or descending order the median is the value of the middle item of the sequence.
For example:

£136   £150   £153   **£155**   £158   £158   £168

£155 is the median value. Because it is the middle value it tells us that 50% of sales are less than £155 and 50% are greater than £155. It is not affected by extreme values. It is calculated by this formula:

$$\text{Median} = \frac{n+1}{2} \text{ where } n \text{ is the number of items.}$$

In the example above $\frac{7+1}{2} = $ the 4th item.

When there is an even number of items, e.g. $\frac{8+1}{2}$, the median is the 4th item, usually calculated as the average of the 4th and 5th items.

For example: 7, 12, 17, 19, 23, 32

The value of the median is $\frac{6+1}{2} = $ the 3rd item,

so the average of the 3rd and 4th items is $\frac{17+19}{2} = 18$

Mode

This is the number, value or item that occurs most often in the population. It is the most fashionable or popular and in the example provided for the mean value of sales above is £158. It is known as the **modal value**. The mode is not affected by extreme values.

The mode is particularly useful in market research. Look at this example on the reliability of cars:

> **Note!**
>
> A 'mod' was a young person in the 1960s who wore fashionable clothes.

Totally unreliable	Often breaks down	Satisfactory	Rarely breaks down	Totally reliable
3	7	11	14	2

We can draw this as a vertical bar chart (Figure 18):

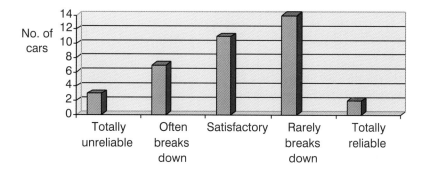

Figure 18 A vertical bar chart based on modal value

The mode or most frequent response is the highest column or bar, 'Rarely breaks down'. Neither the arithmetic mean or median could be used for this analysis.

CTIVITY

Find the mode of the data in the activity on page 60. Is it the same as the mean? Which one would an advertiser use to claim 'Most people spend *x* amount'?

Note!

The sample average is used to predict the population average.

There are three separate values for the average of sales. In our example the mean = £154, the median = £155 and the mode = £158. Choosing which one to use would depend on the objective of the analysis, e.g. management may want staff to work harder and claim average sales are £154 (mean value), staff who are paid on a commission basis would use the mode (£158).

CTIVITY

Can you think of other occasions where various averages might be used? Table 26, which shows the advantages and disadvantages of each method, will help with your decision.

Table 26 *When should each average be used?*

	Advantages	Disadvantages
Mean	Widely known; uses all values; can be used for further analysis	Only useful with numerical data; extreme values can distort
Median	Not affected by extremes; good when a 50/50 split is useful, e.g. wages data	Only useful with numerical data; cannot be used for further analysis
Mode	Can be used for numerical and non-numerical data; shows most popular category	Cannot be used for further analysis

 CACI PayCheck, page 23

Table 27 *When to use different averages*

Checklist	Average to use
Do you want the most popular value?	Mode, e.g. best-selling item
Do you want the middle value?	Median
Do you want to use more statistics?	Mean
Do you want to include extreme values?	Mean
Is the data non-numerical, e.g. categories?	Mode
Is the range small?	Mean, mode
Is the range large?	Median, mode

Frequency distribution/tally chart

This is a table which shows how data is spread or distributed. Table 28 shows some data on the number of complaints received by a company every day in February. Creating a table or frequency distribution will turn the data into information.

Note!

To analyse data construct a frequency distribution; this is a table showing the frequency of a set of values.

Table 28 Number of complaints received by a company every day in February

2	5	3	3	7	4	5
3	1	3	1	2	8	7
9	3	4	2	3	5	6
6	3	4	3	5	3	3

We can do this manually – hand counting – using a tally chart, e.g. on how many days was there one complaint, on how many days were there two complaints, etc (see Table 29).

Table 29 Tally chart of complaints received by a company every day in February

Number of complaints (x)	Tally	Frequency (f) (no of days)	fx (column 1 × column 3)	Cumulative frequency
1	11	2	2	2
2	111	3	6	2 + 3 = 5
3	1111 1111	10 median and mode	30	5 + 10 = 15
4	111	3	12	15 + 3 = 18
5	1111	4	20	18 + 4 = 22
6	11	2	12	22 + 2 = 24
7	11	2	14	24 + 2 = 26
8	1	1	8	26 + 1 = 27
9	1	1	9	27 + 1 = 28
		Total f = 28	Total fx = 113	

The three averages

The **mode** is the value with the largest frequency. In the example above there are three complaints.

The **mean** is calculated as follows:

$$\frac{\text{Sum or total of the } fx \text{ column}}{\text{Sum or total of the } f \text{ column}} = \frac{113}{28} = 4.04$$

The **median** is the value (number of complaints) of the $\frac{28 + 1}{2}$

or 14½th item (day), i.e. the average of the 14th and 15th days. Using the cumulative frequency column, these days are in the class with three complaints. The cumulative frequency column is used instead of writing out the data in ascending order.

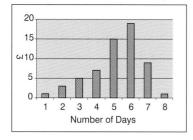

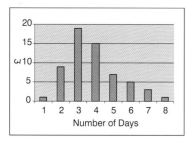

Figure 19 Range of distribution for sales made by a shop over 7 days

Figure 20 The four quartiles

Measures of dispersion

These statistics look at the whole distribution of values and when combined with an average give a good indication of the spread or limits of the data.

The range

This is the difference between the lowest and highest values in a distribution. Here are the sales made by a shop over seven days:

£158   £168   £158   £150   £153   £155   £136.

The range is £168 – £136 = £32. This is a quick, simple and easy statistic, however, it can be very deceptive. For example, look at the two distributions in Figure 19. They both have the same range but the data is distributed differently.

The identification of the extremes used to find the range is particularly helpful in market research, e.g. the highest and lowest selling brands in a store.

Quartiles

These divide a distribution into four equal parts or four groups with equal frequencies (see Figure 20).

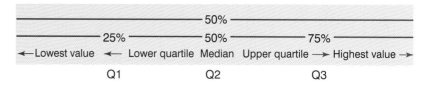

The lower quartile (Q1):
- 25% of items will have values less than Q1.
- 75% will have values more than Q1.
- The position of Q1 is shown by $\frac{n+1}{4}$.

The upper quartile (Q3):
- 25% of the items will have values more than Q3.
- 75% will have values less than Q3.
- Its position is shown by $\frac{n+1}{4} \times 3$.

The median (Q2):
- 50% will have values more than the median.
- 50% will have values less than Q2.
- Its location is shown by $\frac{n+1}{2}$.

If 23 items are arranged in ascending order of value then:
- Q1 is the value of the $\frac{23+1}{4} = $ 6th item.

- The median or Q2 value is $\dfrac{23 + 1}{2} = 12$th item

- Q3 is the value of the $\dfrac{23 + 1}{4} = 6$th item $\times 3 = 18$th item.

Here are the sales for a local shop arranged in ascending order:

£136   £150   £153   **£155**   £158   £158   £168

$Q1 = \dfrac{n + 1}{4} = \dfrac{7 + 1}{4} = 2$nd item $= £150$.

Median or Q2 $= £155$.
Q3 $= £158$.

CTIVITY

Here are 16 customers' purchases at a local shop:
£27, £15, £34, £41, £7, £18, £52, £14, £21, £34, £75, £48, £11, £37, £3, £46.

Tasks

1   Calculate the mean, median, mode, range, lower quartile and upper quartile of this distribution. Use your results to describe the distribution, e.g. 75% of customers spend more than £x.
2   Which is the most appropriate average or measure of dispersion? Give reasons for your choice.

How to do this activity in Microsoft Excel
(see Figure 21)

1   Enter the 16 purchases in column A. These will be the array.
2   Click Insert, then click Function.
3   On the left-hand column click Statistical.
4   On the right-hand column click Quartile.
5   Highlight the array, which will appear as A1:A16 in the Array box.
6   The 'Quart' box allows you to calculate the lower quartile – enter 1, for the median enter 2, and for the upper quartile enter 3 (see screen on following page).
7   For the arithmetic mean click Average in the right-hand column.
8   For the mode click Mode in the right-hand column.

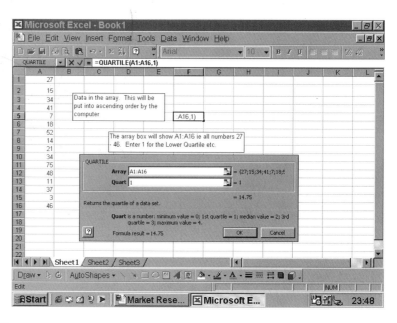

Figure 21 Calculating mean, median and mode in Microsoft Excel

Percentages

Percentages are frequently used and quoted in market research, e.g. Esprit has 20% of the market, sales have risen by 40%. They are probably the most useful way of showing how a distribution is split between various categories (see Table 30). Look at this example.

How to calculate a %:

$$\frac{\text{The part or fraction}}{\text{Value of the whole}} \times 100$$

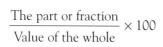

Figure 22 Pie chart of percentages

Table 30 Percentages of users for various types of bean

Product	Number of users	Percentage
Chilli beans	15 (part or fraction)	15/50 x 100 = 30%
Has beans	30	30/50 x 100 = 60%
Thai beans	5	5/50 x 100 = 10%
	Total 50 (whole)	

This information can now be presented as a pie chart or pictogram, as in Figure 22.

A CTIVITY

1 A market research company has obtained these results from an advertising recall survey (people who instantly remember an advert without any prompting).

Product	Number of people	Percentage
Kit Kat	90	?%
Choko	10	?%
Snickers	60	?%
Marathon	40	?%
	200	100%

Calculate the percentage split and present the information as a chart or diagram.

2 Percentages are frequently used to calculate the market share that a brand has in a market. Calculate the market share for each brand from the results of a survey below:

Gap	190
Next	280
River Island	260

How to do it in Microsoft Excel

In column A put in the products. In column B put in the number of people. Highlight A1, A5, B1, B5. Click on Insert, click Chart, then click the type of chart you need (not all will be suitable, however good they look). Follow the on-screen instructions to give your chart a title and label the axes.

Calculating percentage changes

Table 31 shows the number of people who were able to instantly recall an advert. The research was carried out on behalf of Snickers which had advertised heavily during August. What conclusions can you draw?

Table 31 Percentage change in number of people able to instantly recall an advert

Product	No. of people Aug	Sept	Actual change	Calculation	% change
Kit Kat	110	90	−20	20/110 x 100	−18%
Choko	5	10	5	5/5 x 100	100%
Snickers	40	60	20	20/40 x 100	50%
Marathon	45	40	−5	5/45 x 100	−11%
	200	200	0		

For Snickers:

$$\frac{\text{Actual change}}{\text{Original}} = \frac{60\ (\text{Sept}) - 40\ (\text{Aug})}{40\ (\text{Aug})} = \frac{20}{40} \times 100\% = 50\%$$

CTIVITY

Table 32 shows the figures for household food consumption, 1986–2000. This is secondary data.

Table 32 *Figures for household consumption of various food items, 1986–2000*

Year	'86	'87	'88	'89	'90	'91	'92	'93	'94	'95	'96	'97	'98	'99	2000
Fish	146	144	143	147	144	139	142	144	145	144	154	146	146	144	143
Butter	64	61	57	50	46	44	41	40	39	36	39	38	39	37	39
Marg.	116	113	108	98	91	89	79	70	43	41	36	26	26	20	21
Sugar	228	212	196	183	171	167	156	151	144	136	144	128	119	107	105

Source: www.statistics.gov.

Note: units = grams per person per week. Marg. = margarine.

Task

Calculate the percentage change in consumption for each product between 1986 and 2000. What conclusions can you make about changes in diet? Can you suggest why the changes have taken place?

> **Note!**
> Percentages that have been calculated for a sample can be applied to the population providing the sample is representative.

> **Note!**
> Time series analysis can be used for weekly, monthly or quarterly (seasonal) data.

Time series analysis

A time series is a run of historical data which shows how the value of a variable changes over time, e.g. household food consumption.

A time series can be analysed to find the underlying trend and to make forecasts.

Finding a trend using moving averages

The first step in analysing a time series is to isolate and define the trend.

Table 33 *Time series analysis of household consumption of butter, 1986–2000*

	'86	'87	'88	'89	'90	'91	'92	'93	'94	'95	'96	'97	'98	'99	2000
Butter	64	61	57	50	46	44	41	40	39	36	39	38	39	37	39
3-year moving total		182	168	153	140	131	125	120	115	114	113	116	114	115	
3-year moving average or trend		61	56	51	47	44	42	40	38	38	38	39	38	38	
Variation		0	1	−1	−1	0	−1	0	1	−2	1	−1	1	−1	

Opposite is a graph of the consumption of butter in grams per person per week, which gives a visual impression of the data (see Figure 23).

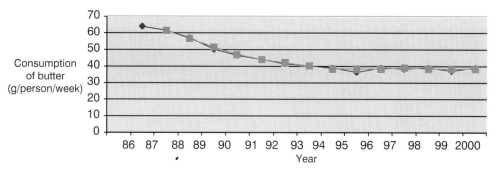

Figure 23 *A graph showing consumption of butter in grams per person per week*

Step 1: Calculate the moving total

Calculate a three-year moving total using the data in row 2 of Table 34:

Table 34 *Calculation of a three-year moving total for household butter consumption*

1986 + 1987 + 1988 = 64 + 61 + 57 =	182
1987 + 1988 + 1989 = 61 + 57 + 50 =	168
1988 + 1989 + 1990 = 57 + 50 + 46 =	153

The total 'moves' by deleting the first year and adding the subsequent year. The total is placed in row 3. The first total is 182, which is inserted against 1987, i.e. the middle year (it is the total of three years). Do this for each successive three years. The totals are shown in row 3.

Step 2: Calculate the moving average

Calculate a three-year moving average by dividing row 3 by 3 (years) to find the trend, e.g.

$$\frac{182}{3} = 60.6 \text{ rounded up} = 61$$

$$\frac{168}{3} = 56$$

The figures are shown in row 4; repeat this step for each total. This is the trend: the consumption of butter fell steadily from 1987 to 1994, and it was relatively stable from 1994 to 2000. The year 2000 is the latest year available.

A pack of butter weighs 250 grams. How much does your family buy in a week? Do you use more or less than the 'average' person?

> If a higher level of detail is needed it may be necessary to work to 1 decimal place, e.g. $\frac{182}{3} = 60.6$, or 2 decimal places $= 60.67$.

Step 3: Calculate the variation

The variation shows the amount by which the actual data varies from the underlying trend. It is calculated using this formula:

Actual data – Trend = Variation.

This is shown in row 5. The variation in this example is small, with a maximum of 2 grams.

ACTIVITY

Use the time series data (page 68) to calculate the trend for the consumption of sugar. What conclusions can you draw?

Variation

Variation can be due to other factors that vary through time, for example seasonal variation (e.g. changes in the number of ice-creams sold throughout the year due to changes in the weather) or weekly variation (e.g. a shop's total sales may be much higher at weekends, when the shop is busier than during the week; Table 35). The second example is shown below:

Table 35 *Weekly variation in sales*

	Actual sales	Trend	Variation	
Friday	45	35	10	
Sat	50	35	15	Actual sales higher than trend
Sun	49	35	14	
Mon	30	36	−6	Actual sales are lower

Many of the government's time series use quarterly data (look at the *Monthly Digest of Statistics*); a four-quarterly moving average is used to identify the trend.

Forecasting

The purpose of many market research surveys is to forecast or predict the expected demand for a product. Forecasts are made for a particular period of time:

- short term, e.g. monthly
- medium term – usually one to two years
- long term – three to five years.

Opposite is an example of a forecast made by Keynote for the UK food market.

There are two main categories of forecasting: qualitative ('qual') and quantitative ('quant').

Qualitative methods of forecasting

This method uses the views and opinions of a range of stakeholders when forecasting.

Client and customer surveys

With this method, a business will survey its buyers to find out what they expect to be ordering over the next 12 to 18 months. Although the

> ## Forecasts to 2005
> There is also the likelihood of some downturn in the economy, which may have a negative impact on sales in some of the expanding premium segments of the market. Sales are forecast to increase by 7.8% at current prices.
>
> Socio-economic influences on the market will include the ageing population and the increasing numbers of single-person households and working women. Convenience foods and snack-based foods will continue to be growth areas. Health foods and organic foods are likely to become more prominent, and more time-starved shoppers will turn to Internet-based grocery shopping for their major weekly purchases, topping these up with visits to local stores.
>
> Source: Keynote Executive Summary UK Food Market

method is also popular with both the CBI and government departments who publish regular reports on buyers' expectations, it does have problems:

- buyers may be reluctant to reveal their intentions
- buyers might not know their future demands.

Useful information on the level of future orders and the level of current stocks is available from the Business Monitor series published by HMSO and the ONS.

Sales staff surveys

Although this method appears sensible, in practice, as any sales representative will tell you, there are problems. One sales representative, who did not wish to be named, said:

'Whenever the sales management team are carrying out a survey to try and estimate next year's sales, say you don't know, or say you have several leads but can't be certain. When our company did a staff survey and found sales were expected to be pretty buoyant, they tried to change the commission we got on sales. We will never tell them anything again.'

The Delphi method

This method is named after a famous oracle (wise person) who lived in Delphi, a city in Ancient Greece. It involves asking a group of experts to look into the future to predict major trends. For example, it is suggested that books and literacy will become more important as computers demand high levels of reading skills. Experts, however, can be expensive, and it could be cheaper for the business to join a trade or research association which specialises in its products, in order to get its information.

Managerial expertise

Whatever research data is collected it will be necessary for the management team to use its knowledge and expertise to analyse it. Professional judgement can still be better than computer prediction.

Quantitative methods of forecasting

These methods are usually purely numerical and work using historical or 'back data' time series.

Using Microsoft Excel to make forecasts (see Figure 24)

1 Input the time, e.g. weeks, months or years, in column A. This is the independent variable, which would be shown on the horizontal or x-axis on a graph.
2 Input the sales or other variable in column B. This is the dependent variable (i.e. sales depend on time), which would be shown on the vertical or y-axis on the graph.
3 Go to Insert, Function, Statistical, Forecast.
4 In the box for X enter the date, week number, etc. Do not enter the cell number.
5 Known Xs – highlight the A column/array by holding down the left-hand button on the mouse.
6 Known Ys – highlight the B column/array by holding down the left-hand button on the mouse.
7 The forecast will be shown.

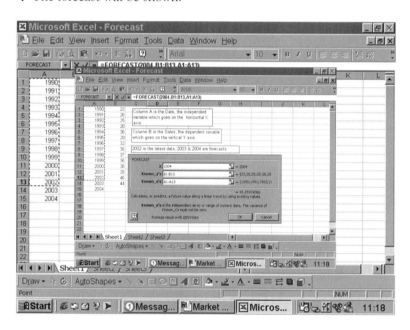

Figure 24 *Using Microsoft Excel to make forecasts*

Using time series data to make forecasts

To make a forecast the trend line must be extended to the right. This process (called **extrapolation**) will give an estimate of the trend for perhaps one or two years ahead, provided that the same set of conditions apply and no major changes occur. To forecast an actual value use this formula:

Actual forecast value = Forecast trend value + 'Seasonal' variation (see Figure 25).

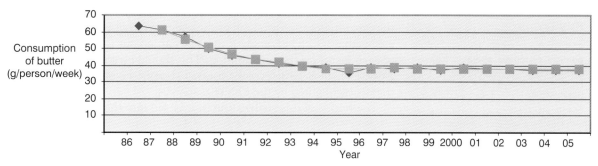

Figure 25 *Forecast consumption of butter to 2005 in grams per person per week*

An interval estimate of between 37 and 39 would appear to be a sensible way of forecasting in this situation where there is no clear pattern of seasonal variation. We have assumed that the most recent trend will continue and that the variation would be between +1 and –1.

CTIVITY

Produce a forecast using the information in Table 36. (It is normal to assume that the variation from one year will continue into the next.)

Table 36 *Forecast for household butter consumption for 2003*

	Quarter	Trend	Variation	Forecast value
2002	1	90	+11	
	2	90	–2	
	3	91	–9	
	4	92	+13	
2003	1	93		
	2	93		
	3	94		
	4	94		

This technique is quantitative, i.e. purely mathematical. It uses historical patterns and trends (time series), but does not include any environmental factors in the forecast. At the time when a forecast is required some qualitative assessment needs to be made. For example, the demand for supermarket fruit and vegetables varies with the weather and the recipes used by TV chefs. The Met. Office now produces general seasonal forecasts which look three to four months ahead!

ACTIVITY

How might a supermarket such as Sainsburys or Morrisons use such a Met Office forecast? Would you rely on it?

'Bring round a few friends, do a bit of italian salad, pour on a very generous amount of basil-enhanced sun dried tomatoes drenched in extra virgin first cold-pressed olive oil, sit back and watch the shelves empty.'

Note!

www.statistics.gov **has long runs of time series data and datasets.**

Writing in the sixteenth century, Nostradamus is alleged to have prophesied/predicted many of the major world events.

Each way betting means putting a bet on a horse so that you win something if it comes in or is placed 1st, 2nd, or 3rd.

Long-term strategic forecasts that determine the future direction of the organisation need to look at the wider external environment. This means that a PESTEL analysis must be carried out to assess the impact of each factor on the organisation. This should be combined with a SWOT analysis, which can be used to identify the opportunities and threats highlighted by the PESTEL analysis.

The results of this analysis can now be fed into the forecasting process.

Problems with forecasts

- How much data does the business have? Generally the more data a business possesses the more reliable will be the forecast, e.g. a longer time series or larger sample should be more reliable.
- Will the external environment remain the same? For example, significant changes in the PESTEL factors could prove to be new opportunities or threats. Random or totally unpredicted events such as the attack on the 'Twin Towers' on 11 September 2001 can cause even the most carefully researched forecast to fail. British Airways was forced to lay off thousands of workers as passenger numbers fell. The predicted revenues of the new National Air Traffic Control System were much lower than anticipated (at the time of writing it was near bankruptcy). Whereas, on the other hand, the budget no frills airlines such as Easyjet appear to have suffered less.
- Will the internal environment remain the same, for example, will the business keep the same objectives or pursue the same policies? Will key staff who have contributed to past success leave or stay?
- Is there enough data for the forecast to be a reliable guide? Is the data representative and unbiased? Is it accurate, up to date and complete?
- The longer ahead the forecast is, the less likely it is to be accurate, particularly in a dynamic/rapidly changing environment. For this reason forecasters may sometimes quote a range of figures (an interval estimate). For example, sales can be expected to be between 26,500 (an upper limit) and 26,000 (a lower limit) units, instead of 26,250 (point estimate). Think of it this way, 'I predict that my examination grade will be between 0–100'; your forecast will be totally accurate and utterly useless! Give yourself credit, forecast between 60–70%, you are less likely to be right, but it is much more helpful!
- Does the business have sufficient intelligence on its competitors? What assumptions can it make about their behaviour?

Significance

This concept describes how closely a sample relates to the population from which it is taken. We sample to find out about the population. For example, has consumer awareness of the product improved after an advertising campaign? The problem we are faced with is whether or not the sample we have chosen is a reliable representative guide.

We start from the assumption that no change has occurred in consumer awareness; this is called the **null** or **no change situation/hypothesis**.

We now carry out our sample survey, the results show that there has been a change. However, is this due to a poor sample or does it mean that there has in fact been a change in consumer awareness of the brand? An alternative sample might show no change in consumer awareness, does this mean there was no change or again is it a poor sample? Look at the following example:

A company carries out a monthly sample to calculate its market share. The results have always been between 9.5% and 10.5%. However this month the result is 6%. Is this significant? Is the result a fluke due to poor sampling or a sign that market share has actually fallen? The company could sample again or wait until next month. Deciding when a result is significant and worth further investigation is an important management decision. Making sure that a sample is always as accurate as possible is one way of reducing the problem.

> **Note!**
>
> Using random samples where every item has a known chance of being selected (the probability is known) helps the researcher with decisions about what is/is not a significant result.

ACTIVITY

'Get Fleeced'

Figure 26 below shows the results of the survey using the questionnaire on page 29.

Do you take part in any sports?

1 Yes [50]   No [10]

2 Keeping fit [10]   Swimming [8]
   Walking [7]   Racket sports [3]
   Team sports [12]   Golf [1]
   Indoor games [6]   Other [3]
   Other sports: Sailing, Snowboarding, Skiing

3 How old are you? Please tick.
   15–24 [26]   25–34 [13]   35–44 [9]
   45–54 [5]   55–64 [4]   65+ [3]

4 Which of these brands have you bought during the last year?
   Nike [13]   Adidas [17]   Reebok [7]
   Ellesse [8]   Timberland [5]   Other [10]

5 Which of these sports items are you most likely to purchase in the next three months?
   Fleece [11]   Tracksuit [14]   Waterproofs [4]
   T-shirts [13]   Football kit [6]   Swimwear [11]
   Golf [3]   Tennis [3]   Footwear [15]

6 When you visit a sports shop, which of the following do you think is important? Please tick.

   There were no clear cut answers although value for money, range of brands and quality all scored well.

7 How much do you normally spend?

Under £20	8	£20–40	21	£41–60	11
£61–80	9	£81–100	7	£101+	4

8 We intend to offer a range of extra services. How important do you rate each of these? Please tick the box.

	First choice			Last choice
	1	2	3	4
Hire of equipment	30			
Testing equipment before purchase	16			
Restringing tennis rackets	3			57
Selling sports tickets	11			

9 Where do you usually shop for sports clothing and footwear and why?

   This produced a range of answers from well-known high street names, such as Foot Locker, to relative unknowns, e.g. Athlete's Foot. Brands were popular with everyone. (*Perhaps the question should have asked why they would visit a new sports shop. This should have been picked up in the pre-test/pilot.*)

10 Do you ever watch football on TV?

   Yes 39   No 21

   (*This question should not have been included. It adds nothing to the specific objectives of this survey. Always beware of the temptation to ask too many questions.*)

11 Do you agree that a new sports shop would be a good idea?

   Yes 50   No 10

   (*This was a leading question. Most psychological research shows that the word 'agree' produces agreement while 'disagree' produces disagreement. The question is technically invalid and should be ignored!*)

Figure 26 *Results of the 'Get Fleeced' questionnaire*

Tasks

1 How should this data be presented? Give your reasons and draw suitable charts.

2 Analyse the results for each question; use the information (averages, percentages, dispersions, etc.) to give a brief description of the results of the survey. What conclusions can be drawn?

3 Some of the results are missing: how has this affected your conclusions? Could any decisions be made?

4 How might the seasons affect the results to questions 2 and 5?

5 What is the mode in questions 5, 7 and 8?

6 Can you say what brands/items should be stocked?

7 Has the survey achieved the original objectives?

8 What was missing from the end of the questionnaire?

9 What is the median age of those surveyed?

10 Why have the full results for question 9 not been given?

Presentation and evaluation of data

Reviewing the quality of data

An essential part of any market research is to review and evaluate the quality of the data that has been collected. It is only worthwhile carrying out market research if it is cost effective, i.e. the expected benefits are greater than the cost of acquiring the data. Small businesses should not spend thousands on market research if they are not prepared or capable of acting on the results, e.g. a small local business making savoury pies 'made and sold fresh everyday' would probably be unable to expand into another region unless it was prepared to invest £000s. Very often the results are the opposite of what the client is expecting to hear. It is essential that the initial brief given to the researcher is clearly thought out and agreed. Market research helps with decision making; it does not make decisions; the researcher is not paid to make the decisions about … whether to go ahead with a new product launch unless this is clearly written into the original brief. However, some clients will specifically ask for recommendations.

Here is a checklist that will help with reviewing the data that has been collected:

> **Note!**
>
> To obtain a Grade A you must be able to evaluate how the data was collected and analysed and recommend the next steps that need to be taken by a business. Evaluation means judging or assessing the value of the research, its strengths and weaknesses.

> **A business should not pay for something which it already knows or cannot do anything about.**

1 Did we ask the right questions, have we got the data we wanted? Always pilot or test out questions before the survey is carried out in the marketplace.
2 Is the data complete, i.e. are all segments of the population represented?
3 Is the data accurate and reliable, e.g. if people were questioned at another time would the results be the same?
4 Have enough people been questioned? Is the sample size large enough to generate acceptable results that can be relied on to make a decision?
5 Is the sample free from bias, i.e. were people correctly selected?
6 Have all deadlines been met?
7 Were the right questions asked and was the right data collected to obtain answers to the original brief?
8 Was the right sample selected, or would another sampling method have given better results?
9 Would another research method give more reliable results?
10 Can we justify each part of the research, i.e. why a particular method was chosen and others rejected?

Presentation of results

> **Note!**
>
> Always rehearse slide shows or face-to-face presentations. Check that nothing can go wrong – £000s could be involved.

This is where the results of a survey are brought together and presented to a third party, the audience, e.g. the client or the person who commissioned or paid for the research (or even your group!).

A presentation will need to be well thought out, attractive and interesting but above all well researched. Use a computer package such as PowerPoint for animating your slides, be innovative, create charts and graphs, use a consistent style. Keep It Short and Simple (KISS). Do not overcrowd slides. Look and act professional!

Presentations will usually be based on a full written report. A good report will:

> **Note!**
>
> Set objectives that are SMART, i.e. Specific, Measurable, Achievable, Relevant, and Time-constrained.

- set out the objectives that are to be achieved
- follow a logical structure with page numbers
- cover all aspects of the research survey
- use formal business language, i.e. not chatty and informal (remember this is written for a client)
- be well produced.

Structure of the report

1 **Title page:** title of the report; who it is written for; name of the researcher/company; date.
2 **Contents page**.
3 **Executive summary:** (this is usually the only part of commercially produced reports that is free). It should contain the main findings and recommendations.
4 **Introduction:** terms of reference, i.e. what the researcher was asked to do; the objectives and purpose of the research; what you are trying to achieve – your aims; the deadline.

5 **Procedure:** this section should detail how the information was collected, e.g:

- A questionnaire was constructed and piloted/pre tested
- The sample frame was …
- A stratified sample based on age was used because …
- A survey was carried out when? where? how?
- 85 questionnaires were given out to …
- In-depth interviews were held with …
- Secondary data used was:
  – government sources (give names)
  – commercial sources (give names)
- Refer the reader to your references section.

6 **Findings – analysis and results:** this section of the report should give the main findings of the research as a series of numbered headings. Keep any of your ideas/opinions to the next section. Make this section factual:

- Calculate percentages, averages, dispersion, time series trends, forecasts, etc.
- Construct tables, graphs and charts for your primary and secondary data.
- Construct a tally chart of all the replies to your questions. For example, a questionnaire about trainers worn by students might provide this data. A pie chart or horizontal bar chart would also work well (see Figure 27).

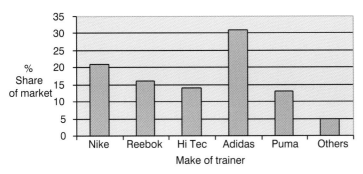

Your findings would be: 'The mode or most popular trainer is Adidas (31%). The majority of people (95%) wore just five brands of trainers. Only 5% wore 'other' trainers, including own labels.' Secondary sources for research into trainers might be:

- Keynote report (UK Sports Market).

> … 'the vast majority of running shoes have never seen a running track, the marketing of a brand is an extremely complex blend of promoting the abilities of the shoe, while publicising the brand'.

Adidas appears to have grown ahead of Nike and new brands such as New Balance have entered the market.

> **If someone or something is 'in the frame' it has a chance of being selected.**

> **Note!**
> Keep back-up copies of everything. In business you cannot say 'I have forgotten my disk' or that the computer has crashed!

 Tally chart, page 63

Figure 27 *A vertical bar chart showing percentage of market held by each make of trainer*

> **Note!**
> Look at commercial market research reports such as Mintel or Keynote for an alternative approach to dealing with a whole market sector, such the 'UK Sports Market' published by Keynote.

- Government statistics
  These are taken from www.statistics.gov, e.g. consumer expenditure 'clothing and footwear'.

7 **Conclusions:** this section should summarise the major findings of your primary and secondary research with a discussion and conclusions.
A checklist of what to include is shown in Table 37:

Table 37 Stages in planning and implementing a questionnaire

Planning stage	• Were the original (SMART) objectives clearly set and achieved?	• Was the questionnaire tested?	• Was the sample frame satisfactory?
Questionnaire	• Did the questionnaire work for all segments?	• Were there enough 'close interview' points?	• What are its strengths and weaknesses?
Sample method	• Was the sample large enough/representative/ the right choice?	• How many people refused?	• Were there problems?
Collection of data	• Was the right method chosen? • Were all segments represented?	• What were its strengths/ weaknesses? • Is data reliable?	• What extra could you do?
Analysis of data	• Which methods were chosen and why?	• Can the information be used for the purpose intended?	• Can the results be used for recommendations and further action?

> **Note!**
>
> Link recommendations to your total knowledge of business, marketing, personnel, financial and production implications. Make them feasible.

8 **Recommendations:** this section should cover the main and subsidiary actions that need to be carried out next; be precise, specific and realistic and apply them totally to the client business. For example:

- Carry out further research such as an alternative method to obtain qualitative data.
- Conduct further analysis to find the quartiles, such as '75% of customers can be expected to spend between £15 and £20'.
- Act on the research findings, e.g. a local newsagents could consider a delivery service, 'Get Fleeced' could hire out equipment (providing expected cost is less than expected revenue). Changing each element of the marketing mix price, promotion, product and place could be included if the research was sufficiently thorough.
- Link primary research to secondary data found in Keynote or Mintel market reports, e.g. primary research suggests that a new sports shop would be viable: the Keynote report 'UK Sports Market' shows that at 23% 'fleece separates' are the biggest seller, not football replica kit!

9 **Acknowledgements:** say thank you to all the organisations and people who may have helped you. Include your family and friends, it is always appreciated. Include any copyrights you may have used.

10 **References:** list all the sources that have been used, both hard and electronic copy. Include author, publisher, web address, date, etc. Remember the client will want to check the sources for reliability and perhaps repeat the survey at a later date to investigate changes in the market.

11 **Appendix:** include the questionnaire and other support materials that have been used. Label them so that they can be referred to in the text.

**CTIVITY**

Write up your final report using the structure given above.
Good Luck!

> **Note!**
>
> This can also be used for the Marketing core unit.

Constraints on market research

At the end of this section you will know about the constraints that exist when carrying out market research, namely – time, money, expertise and ethical issues including privacy, anonymity, confidentiality and safety of the researcher. Legal issues concerned with the Data Protection Act and codes of practice for market research will also be considered. Finally we look at the validity of the sample and the reliability of the data which has been collected. Constraints influence the way researchers work, whom and how they interview, how they keep data secure and how they present results.

Time, money and expertise

Market research is intended to answer immediate questions so deadlines are important; with large surveys many researchers are needed, and this is expensive. Every survey needs to balance the deadline against the cost of achieving it. The client cannot have both unless it is prepared to pay. The deadline is a constraint, the cost is a constraint, the number of researchers available is a constraint.

Ethical issues – privacy, anonymity, confidentiality

Acting or behaving ethically means doing what you know is right. The Market Research Society says 'members shall at all times act honestly with respondents, clients, (actual or potential) employers, employees, sub-contractors and the general public', i.e. all stakeholders in questionnaire design (the website gives other examples).

- Respondents must be openly and honestly informed about the purpose and use of the data that is to be collected.
- Respondents must be openly asked for consent (vital for the Data Protection Act; see opposite).

To ensure that respondents' anonymity is maintained any private information which could be used to identify them must be safeguarded.

As a result of the Data Protection Act 1998 (DP Act) the Market Research Society has produced a new definition of 'classic' survey (or market) research. It includes the sentence:

'The process guarantees the confidentiality of personal information in such a way that the data can only be used for research purposes.'

(www.marketresearch.org)

'Classic' covers both qualitative and quantitative research. Confidentiality is the key word.

As market research relies entirely on the willingness of people to answer the researchers' questions, whether face-to-face, through questionnaires, via the Internet or telephone, the need to operate ethically and legally is vital to maintain trust and integrity. The guidelines and Codes of Practice issued by the Market Research Society (UK) and ESOMAR in Europe pay special attention to the privacy, anonymity and confidentiality of data given by respondents. It is equally important that other wider marketing research is also legal and ethical; this is particularly important with competitor research. Everyone concerned with the research process, the client, the data collection agency and the researcher/interviewer needs to be fully aware of their responsibilities under the DP Act and the rights of respondents. The key decision is whether or not to collect personal data because it is only personal data that is covered by the legislation. In practice, maintaining an ethical position in research is not easy; compromises often need to be made.

> **Note!**
>
> The same ethical issues apply whether the respondent is an individual or the research is business to business.

> **Note!**
>
> A stakeholder is any individual or group who has an interest/concern in the affairs of the business.

Competitor research, page 53

'Ethical responsibilities are non-negotiable. But we should be aware that researchers often need to make informed decisions about the trade off between rigour and practicality'.

Source: Market Research Society website

Safety of the researcher

If you are going to carry out research your first priority must always be your own safety.

- Never go alone if it could be dangerous.
- Always research in a safe public place.
- Make sure someone knows where/when you are researching.
- Carry some kind of identification.
- Find out if you need permission or insurance.
- Check all this with your tutor.

The professional Code of Practice also sets out guidelines to ensure the safety of respondents; any abuse of these guidelines will result in disciplinary action by the professional body and possible criminal proceedings.

> **Researchers must take particular care when interviewing children. Guardian or parental consent must always be obtained and topics that might frighten or disturb them should never be discussed.**
> (Source: MRS Guidelines for research among children and young people)

 MRS Guidelines, page 21

The Data Protection Act applied to market research

This section is based on material provided by the Market Research Society at www.marketresearch.org.uk, which also covers the ethical issues above. There are eight data protection principles contained in the Data Protection Act 1998 (see the list below). They are all concerned with the processing of personal data. The Act only applies to data that can identify an individual, e.g. name, address, NI number, e-mail address, telephone number, etc.

Personal data shall be:

1 processed fairly and lawfully
2 obtained for lawful and specified purposes
3 adequate and relevant – not excessive (no unnecessary questions)
4 accurate and kept up-to-date (inaccurate or incomplete data to be erased or put right)
5 not kept longer than is necessary for the purpose for which it was collected
6 processed so as to keep individual data private
7 kept secure against any unauthorised use, accidental loss or damage
8 kept within the European Economic Area and not transferred outside unless similar protection exists.

> **Note!**
> You could avoid the issues covered in the DP Act if you do not collect personal data in any survey you carry out, i.e. if your respondents cannot be identified.

> **Note!**
> The European Economic Area is the European Union plus Norway, Iceland and Liechtenstein, which also have the free movement of services (in this instance data).

How does the DP Act affect market research?

The Act affects market research in two main ways: transparency and consent.

- **Transparency**: individuals must be clearly told why the data is being collected and how it will be used. This applies to all types of questionnaire and interview.

- **Consent**: individuals must agree to their data being collected (i.e. they must be able to refuse) and have the right to opt out of any later use of the data.

The Market Research Society has identified five key stages when the Act applies. These are shown, in simplified version, in Table 38 below:

Table 38 The five key stages of market research when the DP Act applies

Planning and preparation	Client provides sample frame	Data collection	Processing, analysis, reporting & storage	Destruction of the data
Make sure the data is: • secure • properly used • properly disposed of after use.	Security: • How is the data stored, protected, disposed of? • Are the premises secure? • Is the list 'clean', i.e. up to date, accurate?	Make sure the respondent knows: • who the collector is • for whom the data is being collected Make sure that interviewers are briefed on security and DP issues.	Make sure that: everyone concerned with the data: • follows security and storage procedures • is aware that respondents can see data held on them • does not give the data to 'third parties'.	Make sure that: • all hard and electronic copy is held securely • confidentiality is maintained at all times • confidential documents are shredded.

Market Research Society Codes of Practice

Codes of Practice are now available for a range of professions. The Market Research Code of Practice is a set of rules or guidelines created to regulate the industry. It sets standards and acts as a framework for all research activities. It sets out how researchers should behave and act. It is designed to make sure that research is carried out legally and ethically. Because research depends on co-operation, the general public and businesses need to know that their rights to privacy and confidentiality are respected. The Code of Practice covers professional responsibilities, the rights of respondents (e.g. to ensure they are in no way harmed or adversely affected), the rights and responsibilities of clients.

Validity and reliability of the data

The need to ensure that any data, however collected, is valid and reliable means that rigorous quality control checks must be in place for every step of the research process. Questionnaires must be thoroughly tested to make sure that they get the right information, at the right time, from the right people.

1 The main principle governing the writing and phrasing of questions is one of technical best practice – it is the industry's responsibility to generate data that is as close to objectivity as is possible. Researchers must try to make sure that:

- the questions are fit for the purpose and clients are advised accordingly
- the design of the questionnaire is right for the audience being researched
- respondents are able to answer the questions in a way that reflects the view they want to express
- the answers are capable of being interpreted in a meaningful and unambiguous way.

In summary:

- Will the respondents understand the questions?
- Will they be willing to answer the questions?
- Will they be able to answer the questions?

2 In practice every researcher knows that there is no right and wrong question or answer.

Source: Market Research Society

Every effort must be made to ensure that the sample is representative of the target market and free from bias. In practice this will mean:
- checking that the sample frame and sample are accurate and include all segments
- checking that researchers remain objective
- ensuring that any quotas or strata are strictly followed
- ensuring that all data is thoroughly checked
- ensuring that no short cuts are taken, e.g. if 800 people should be interviewed then 800 must be interviewed.

Although this adds to the costs (i.e. it is a constraint), it is the only way to safeguard the integrity of the research industry.

Our qualitative market research

If there are any changes you would like us to make to improve your book, please write to the publisher and let us know.

Roger Lewis and Roger Trevitt

Index